Switch
on
your
brain

Switch on your brain

Margaret Stuart
and
Allan Parker
in collaboration with
Paul E. Dennison, Ph.D.

HALE
& IREMONGER

To Ingrid and Tim,
two very important and special young people
to whom we owe so much

© 1986 Margaret Stuart and Allan Parker
10 9 8 7 6 5 4 3 2

Typeset, printed & bound by
Southwood Press Pty Limited
80-92 Chapel Street, Marrickville, NSW

For the publisher
Hale & Iremonger Pty Limited
GPO Box 2552, Sydney, NSW

National Library of Australia
Cataloguing-in-publication entry:

Stuart, Margaret.
Switch on your brain.

ISBN 0 86806 615 X

1. Kinesiology. 2. Reading. I. Parker, Allan. II.
Dennison, Paul E. (Paul Ehrlich). III. Title.

612.74

Foreword

Education is a cornerstone of personal development. A well-balanced education will give rise to a well-balanced individual who will, in turn, maintain and enhance a well-balanced society. There are many facets of a well-balanced education, the ultimate aim of which should be to groom each individual to be useful to himself or herself and to society. That individual should be able to live in harmony with himself, his fellows, and with all animate and inanimate objects. Our descendants will be the living proof of how successful our education has been.

But, the school system tends to cater for everyone in general and rarely for everyone in particular. Fortunately, many manage to get by. But many do not. They may advance up the educational ladder year by year, but learning becomes a chore rather than a joy, and real education passes them by. It is for these people that Educational Kinesiology offers real hope.

Drawing upon a knowledge of brain process, remedial educational techniques, and even some of the principles of oriental medicine, EK enhances our ability to learn. Moreover, the techniques are easy to follow and no special equipment is required.

An exciting aspect of EK is that the results may sometimes be immediate. As Allan Parker can testify, its procedures can have a profound effect upon the individual. All of us, regardless of how well or badly we feel or perform, can improve our performance and enhance our self esteem.

Dr Douglas Yeoh, M.B., B.S.
Moorebank. N.S.W.

5

Preface

We have both come to Educational Kinesiology (EK) by different paths, yet both of us have found its study and exercises have revolutionised our professional lives: Allan, in his role as naturopath and stress management consultant, solving his own difficulties with learning; and Margaret as a teacher constantly frustrated by the bright student who was not able to achieve potential — who had to work long hours to gain average marks — and by the not-so-bright student who worked even harder to gain minimal marks.

At first sight, EK seems to be hocus-pocus. The idea that running your hand from the pubic area to the bottom lip will make you read better seems just too much to accept. But 'seeing is believing' and now, having seen so many people helped by EK, we are convinced that it is a major breakthrough in education and should be a part of teacher-training programs throughout the world.

People will always be sceptical, and that is as it should be. But if you are wondering whether or not to try EK, ask yourself not 'what if it doesn't work?', but rather 'what if it works?'. We are certain you will be amazed, fascinated and convinced of the limitless benefits of this wonderful technique.

Acknowledgements

We wish to express our deep gratitude to Bill Stuart, Alex, Ro and Norma, Joe Bright, Phillip Crockford, Susan Greer, Eric Robertson, and John Thie, and all those people with whom we have worked and from whom we have learnt so much.

Acknowledgement by Allan Parker

Having experienced a degree of learning difficulties throughout my own schooling years, and the associated effects on my self-esteem and personality, I can understand the hardships which go hand in hand with those difficulties.

I am truly grateful for the hardships which at the time seemed so unpleasant and unfair. For now I can recognise qualities in myself as a person, as an educator, and as a practitioner which are clearly results of those unpleasant times.

I, and hopefully many others, are grateful for the work, love and dedication of Dr Paul Dennison who was responsible for the development of Educational Kinesiology. I am grateful not only for the fact that through his work I have been able to develop but also for his agreeing to us using his material in this book.

To Dr Dennison — my sincerest gratitude.

Contents

What is EK?

Educational Kinesiology is a method of integrating the processes of the right and left halves of the brain to bring about improvement in the ability of the individual to assimilate and recall information, resulting in an increased capacity to learn. The techniques were developed by American educationalist, Dr Paul Dennison. They are not complicated nor do they require any prior knowledge or training.

EK techniques are a major breakthrough in education. Conventional teaching methods often seem to be inadequate or inappropriate to cope with the inability of many people, both children and adults, to learn to read and write fluently.

To improve our ability to learn, both halves of the brain must work together in harmony. When someone has some form of learning difficulty, the two halves either do not communicate with each other to work together as a whole, or one half does far more of the work than the other. When this happens, blocks are created that prevent information getting into or out of the brain and learning difficulties result.

EK techniques identify and locate these blocks. The specific techniques and exercises overcome the blocks and establish a flow of information between both halves of the brain. The techniques improve right and left brain co-ordination and thus assist specific learning methods rather than replace them. The exciting thing about EK is that it shows results in a short period of time, in some cases immediately. It is very safe and can be used by adults, children and teachers alike.

One of EK's strongest features is that it is not just for those people who have overt learning difficulties. Its benefits have been apparent to those who have never seen themselves as having learning problems. It allows the learner not only to improve his skills but also to believe in himself and his ability to improve.

Two analogies

Our nervous system and electricity

Our nervous system is similar to the electrical system in a building. The building has a power or energy supply, as does the body, and built into that power system are circuit breakers designed to prevent the system from overloading. When the system gets to the point of overload, when it might be damaged, the circuit breaker cuts in and reduces, or switches off, the power. Similarly, our bodies have inbuilt circuit breakers to cut in and reduce the energy supply to a stressed area, thus immobilising or inactivating that part.

The purpose of EK techniques is to identify and reduce the stress factors that prevent us functioning efficiently. The techniques allow the restoration of power to the affected area so that we may process information more effectively.

Light and dark

If we enter a room and turn off the light switch we are left in the dark. Someone entering the room and not knowing that the light has been turned off may assume that the electricity system is defective, when in fact it is working perfectly. All that needs to be done is to find the switch and re-establish the power flow.

Similarly, when an area of the brain or nervous system is overloaded or stressed, the switch 'turns off', leaving that area in the dark. The brain ceases to process information properly. For instance, the eyes may not perceive pictures and spaces as well as they might do if the switch were on; the ears will often confuse the messages they receive. The fact that the light in a room or the specific function or process of the brain is not operating does not mean that part of the system is not a good and workable part. It merely means that it is temporarily not functioning.

Just as the light in the room may be restored by turning on the switch, so the brain may be restored to full working capacity once we find out why it is 'switched down'.

Brain Process

The brain is divided into two halves — the left brain or left hemisphere, and the right brain or right hemisphere. These two halves are joined by millions of fibres called the *corpus callosum* through which information passes back and forth from the rest of the body. The left brain controls the right half of the body and the right brain controls the left half of the body.* Each brain handles information differently:

Left brain/hemisphere	Right brain/hemisphere
Logical/Analytical	Integrated/Holistic
Information is processed in a very factual, logical, realistic manner. The left brain recalls the information. What is perceived is broken down into its	The right brain takes the component parts and organises them into a complete image or concept (*gestalt*).

*An excellent book on brain process and function is *Left Brain — Right Brain* by S. Springer & G. Deutsch, Freeman & Co., USA, 1981.

component parts. The left brain does not see these parts as having any relationship to themselves or other parts.

Serial or Sequential

Things are done one at a time, in order. No two things are done in an overlapping or simultaneous fashion.

Parallel

Capable of handling multiple operations, of collecting many pieces of information simultaneously and making patterns.

Focal/Convergent

Focal, meaning that it focuses on minute details and component parts. Again, the left brain sees no relationship to the entirety of the object or unit.

Diffused/Divergent

Diffused or divergent in that the right brain processes on a total scale. Its attention is on the entirety. It integrates the component parts and organises them into a whole. It looks at all aspects simultaneously rather than in isolated detail.

Verbal

The left brain takes in and sends out speech. It is mathematically and numerically oriented.

Visual/Spatial

Receives and delivers visual images. It is pictorial and is also musically oriented and creative.

The left hemisphere is responsible for performing repetitious or similar tasks. The right hemisphere might note the similarity in appearance of a number of objects but would not pay attention to the function or use of those objects.

The left half of the brain controls the right half of the body and its gross and fine motor activity; the right half of the brain controls the left half of the body and its gross and fine motor activity. When the two halves are integrated, the two halves of the physical body are co-ordinated. Conversely, when we co-ordinate the two halves of the physical body we integrate the two halves of the brain.

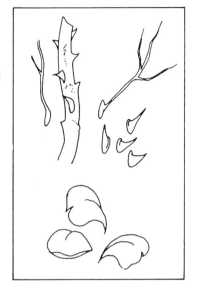 

The left brain would see the components of a rose bush — the thorns, the stems, leaves and petals. The right brain would see the rose bush as a whole and be able to differentiate it from other flower bushes.

Reading

In *reading*, the left half of the brain isolates and identifies the individual syllables or words while the right hemisphere synthesises the component parts, giving meaning to what is being read. Someone who reads with the left half of the brain playing the greater role may emphasise each syllable and hesitate as he reads. For example:

A wri/ter gen/er/ally has some feel/ings to/wards his sub/ject*

Because such a person concentrates on parts of words, he has a poor or reduced understanding of the meaning of what he is reading.

By contrast, a *right brain reader* guesses at words and has a very sing-song voice as he 'reads the rhythm' rather than reads for the meaning of the words.

The excellent reader reads phrases and sentences and is able to understand the meaning, not only of words and phrases, but of sentences and paragraphs, and to piece together those phrases, to draw meaning from them and from the entire sentence, paragraph or chapter. That person reads 'holistically'. The excellent reader reads with both left and right brains working together as an integrated unit.

In the pages that follow we outline the exercises that will enable you to integrate both halves of the brain to make learning both easier and more enjoyable.

Assessment

Before commencing EK, it is best to test your student's reading ability, so that you will later have a yardstick by which to identify improvement.

1. Have the student read aloud. Take notice of the way he reads — whether it is disjointed or fluent.
2. Have the student write several sentences (handwriting and printing). Handwriting requires both halves of the brain to work together; printing involves mainly the left brain.
3. Have the student copy work from a board. (People often can read well but cannot copy.)
4. Test the student's verbal and written spelling ability. Pick a set of 10 or 15 words and have the student spell

---

*From *How to analyse prose — what is the writer saying?* by Margaret Cutler-Stuart, Hale & Iremonger, 1986.

them to you. Record the words that are spelled correctly (not those that are spelled incorrectly). Do not give any feedback or advice as to whether a mistake has been made, simply note the mistake for later reference.

5. Test the student's comprehension. Have him read an article either aloud or to himself, whichever he prefers, and then have him

(a) write down as many things as he can recall from the article, and

(b) answer some specific questions that you have prepared.

These five steps will allow you to identify later improvement.

How to Test Muscles

Introduction

EK uses muscle responses as a way of measuring the effectiveness of the passage of information into and out of the brain via the nervous system. When testing muscles we are not trying to overpower the other person nor to determine how strong that person's muscles are. The muscle test is used to give us vital information about how we are processing or not processing information. It is also used to reassess the changes brought about by the techniques used.

Before a muscle can be used the muscle should be tested to determine its original status. It is important to know whether the muscle originally tested 'switched on' or 'switched off' in order to make this comparison. A switched on muscle is very definitely switched on — there is nothing uncertain about it. So, when we are unsure about a muscle response, we call it switched off.

Switched On	Switched Off
very strong holding power	slow
sharp reflex	moves
automatic reflex	trembles
effortless	some discomfort is felt
	recruiting (i.e., other muscles are called on to help hold the arm)
	entails conscious effort

Muscle testing involves two people co-operating to bring about positive change, so the secondary purpose of muscle testing is to enhance the relationship of the two people using the technique so that they may each help the other to learn.

The muscle being tested is called the indicator muscle no matter which of the four muscles given below is being used.

Before proceeding
Ask the person being tested if he knows any reason it is inadvisable to test a muscle (e.g., injury to a joint or bone). If he feels any pain or discomfort, he is to tell you loudly and clearly so that the testing may stop.

Have the person carry out the following:
1. Drink a glass of water.
2. Rub the ball of his foot and at the same time rub the spot where each toe joins the foot. Do this with both feet.
3. Place one of his fingers on his lower lip and the other on the top of his pubic bone and touch lightly for 20 seconds.

To test a muscle — 'testing in the clear'
1. Ensure that the person does not cross his legs or ankles.
2. Use the **Two F.I.S.** rule when testing:
   use   two **F**ingers to apply the pressure;

move arm   two **I**nches. If the arms moves down more than two inches, consider the muscle switched off;

for   two **S**econds. Apply pressure for *only* two seconds.

3. (a) Have the person say 'PUSH' as you gently push the arm in the direction indicated. Record whether the response is switched on or switched off.

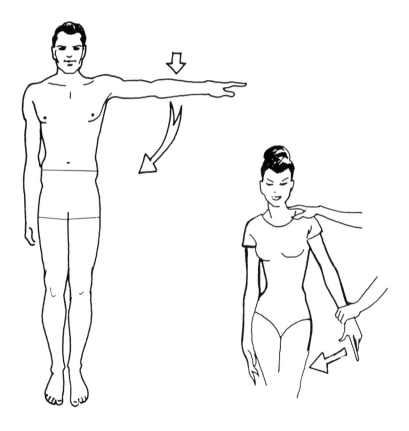

Testing in the clear   *Fig Leaf (Supraspinatus)*

(b) Have the person say 'PUSHHHH' while you pinch lightly anywhere on the body and test the muscle. Record the response.

This is what we call *testing in the clear*. We are assessing the quality of response, not the strength of that part of the body. It is not important to know what response to expect — just do the test and record the reponse.

Muscles to test

The four muscles we use for testing are:

The Fig Leaf *(Supraspinatus muscle — central meridian associated with the brain)*

Extend the arm to 30 degrees diagonally out from the hip. The movement of the arm is towards the 'fig leaf' area of the body. Have the person tell you when he is ready to resist, then push on the arm above the wrist *gently* as he locks his arm to prevent you pushing it down to the fig leaf area.

This particular muscle is associated with what is called in acupuncture the central meridian which is an energy flow from the pubic area up to the centre of the bottom lip. The central meridian is associated with the brain and, therefore, its associated muscle is a very good one to test for brain processing efficiency.

Flyer *(Deltoid — associated with the lung)*

Stand up straight, extend your arm out from the body as if you are going to flap your arm just as a bird would flap its wing. Keep the arm horizontal. Have the person tell you when he is ready to hold, then *gently* push on the arm above the wrist as he locks his arm to prevent you pushing it down to the side of the body.

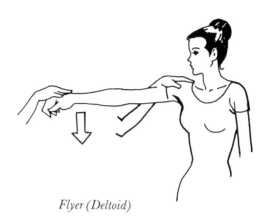

Flyer (Deltoid)

Swimmer *(Pectoralis Major Clavicular — associated with the stomach)*

This performs an action similar to a breast stroke swimming action.

Point the extended arm out in front of you, parallel to the ground. Rotate the arm so that the thumb points to the ground. The movement is down and out at 45 degrees, as though breast stroke swimming. As you gently push on the arm the person holds against your push and locks his arm in place.

Swimmer (Pectoralis Major Clavicular)

Penguin *(Latissimus Dorsi — associated with the spleen)*
This large muscle in
the back brings the
arm from the out-
ward position to
alongside the body.
To test the muscle
extend the arms
down by the body.
Rotate the arm so
that the palm faces
outward. Try to pull
the arm away from
the body as the
person holds or locks
his arm at his side.

Penguin (Latissimus Dorsi)

Trial test
Stand and move your arm out into the Supraspinatus
muscle (Fig Leaf) position as explained and illustrated
above. Your partner stabilises you by placing his hand on
the opposite shoulder to the testing arm. He then holds
your testing forearm above the wrist. Have a practice run
by moving the arm down into the midline or groin area
backwards and forwards several times so that not only the
person doing the test becomes familiar with what needs to
be done but also to allow you, your muscles and your nervous system to get used to what is going to take place.

Then, take up the starting position at 30 degrees up and
out from your body, have your partner's hand on the forearm and, when you are ready, tell your partner to push,
applying pressure to the forearm down in the direction of
the midline. This pressure is light and is best done with two
fingers. It does not need to be heavy pressure. The pressure
simply needs to be sufficient to establish whether the

muscle is responding to stimuli. We are not testing the amount of strength that the muscle has. We are simply testing its ability to respond, to lock in place, and the speed with which it can do that.

Now, advise your partner to push on the arm. Is the response 'switched on' or 'switched off'?

Water

The most elementary and most readily available tool in EK is water, preferably steam distilled.

When testing a person with learning difficulties, find a strong indicator muscle and have the person read. Retest. Have the person drink a glass of water and then have him reread. Often there will be an improvement in his reading. Retest. The muscles may now be switched on. From a physiological point of view, the brain cells, which require large quantities of water to function effectively, will work at a higher level of performance if the body receives sufficient water.

Conversely, loss of concentration and diminished ability to recall information will result when the brain lacks sufficient water.

A simple test for dehydration is to find a strong indicator muscle. Have the person gently pull his hair. Test the muscle. If the body needs water, the muscle will test switched off. Once the body has sufficient water the muscle will test switched on. Always check for dehydration before you start EK exercises. Tea, coffee, fruit juices or mixed beverages do not have the same switching on effect as does plain water.

Reading

Do you . . . ?
- Read sentences one word at a time?
- Sound out the word before you pronounce it aloud?
  (subvocalisation)
- Read with little expression?
- Read in a sing-song manner?
- Read better backwards than forwards?
- Drop off to sleep when reading?
- Read, but retain little of what you have read?
- Find you are easily distracted when you are reading?
- Take up a difficult or distorted posture when you are reading?
- Track the words and lines with your finger as you read?
- Read well but cannot remember what you have read?
- Move your head left to right as you read?
- Read what is written on the left and right of the page but have difficulty seeing what is in the middle, so that you guess at words placed in the centre of the page?
- Read one line, cannot read the next two lines, but then read the fourth line?
- Invent words or letters?

Many people who find reading difficult will answer 'yes' to some of these questions. Below we outline ways in which you may use EK exercises to improve your reading.

Test the four muscles until you get a strong response from one of them. Try the Fig Leaf (Supraspinatus) first.

Cross pattern marching   *Homolateral marching*

Have the person cross pattern march (i.e., simultaneously move right arm/left leg forward then left arm/right leg). In most cases you will find that cross pattern marching for approximately 30 seconds will either maintain or bring about a switching on effect of the muscle.

Now have the person (for approximately 30 seconds) homolaterally march so that the left arm and the left leg move simultaneously, followed by the right arm and the right leg moving together. Retest and note the response.

Have the person read a paragraph and note the characteristics of the reading. Is it fluent, that is, does it flow in an
easy fashion connecting words together with ease, or is it
being performed in a stilted, word-by-word fashion? Test
the muscle response. Now have the person read exactly the
same paragraph but this time he should read it from the
last word backwards through to the first. Again monitor
the fluency with which the passage is read. Retest the muscle and take note of the response.

Reading requires both sides of the brain to work
together to:

1. allow the left half of the brain to identify the component parts and
2. allow the right brain to take those component parts and
   synthesise them, thereby producing words which then
   produce sentences that formulate meaning.*

In someone with a learning difficulty, or with someone
who is a slow reader or has poor concentration or poor
memory, the left half of the brain does most of the work and
the right half is less active. When this occurs reading is
stilted, and words may be broken into syllables and not
identified as a whole. The tone of the voice will be less
expressive and sound monotonous. As a result of this, the
retention and comprehension of the information read will
be poor.

But, reading the words backwards will be done fluently
and quickly. This occurs because when the left hemisphere
is dominating, it identifies the component parts. Reading
backwards removes the stress of putting the words together
to form meaning as we must do when we read forwards.

Physical body responses may also indicate that the person is being stressed by the reading activity. Somebody

---

*Remember when you are studying to give your left brain a rest every 45 minutes to an
hour by listening to music (muscle test the music beforehand to ensure it is keeping you
switched on) and by looking at things in the distance (not TV) — do things that alter-
nate the work load between the predominantly left brain step-by-step work and the right
brain (spatial, diagrammatic, creative) work.

reading forward from the left half of the brain will often have an increased blood supply to the face and become red while parts of the body will start to fidget. When the body becomes stressed, more adrenalin is pumped into the system because its automatic fight or flight response is being activated and movement is the natural response to this.

It is usually apparent when the redness is caused by stress and not by self-consciousness.

Summary
1. Cross pattern march — 30 seconds. (Right arm/left leg simultaneously; left arm/right leg simultaneously.)
   A. Test muscle — note response.
2. Homolateral march (left leg/left arm simultaneously; right arm/right leg simultaneously) — 30 seconds.
   B. Test muscle — note response.
3. Read a paragraph forward — is reading fluent? stilted?
   C. Test muscle — note response.
4. Read the same paragraph backwards — is the reading better?
   D. Test muscle — note response.

The X I I Test

This exercise tests the brain's ability to integrate both halves so that they work together.

1. Draw a cross of approximately 3" in diameter on one piece of paper and on another piece of paper draw two parallel lines of the same size.
2. Muscle test until you establish a strong response.
3. Have the person look at the cross. Muscle test and note the response.
4. Have the person look at the two parallel lines. Muscle test again and note the response.

Somebody who operates successfully out of two halves of the brain when perceiving visual symbols will have a strong or switched on response on the X but will have a switched off response when viewing the parallel lines.

The reason for this is that the cross is two component parts put together to form one symbol. For this to be visually perceived, the two halves of the brain need to be operating.

The two parallel lines are not something that requires an integration and are not necessarily something that requires a fusing of the vision; therefore the muscle will test switched off. This test tells us how the brain is processing information, just as reading forwards and backwards gave us information.

What if the response is switched off for the X and switched on for I I?

The person who has learning difficulties often has a reverse reaction because he prefers to operate out of the left hemisphere; his processing mechanism will be more comfortable viewing the two parallel lines because there is no integration or fusing of the vision required to perceive those two objects and so looking at them will be less stressful for him.

The cross requires integration both visually and cerebrally and will be stressful to the person who operates primarily from one side of the brain. The response will therefore be switched off.

Switching On

These four techniques will increase the likelihood of the two halves of the brain working together and increase the likelihood of the vision of the two eyes being fused so that the response when looking at the X will be strong.

1. The Zipper exercise

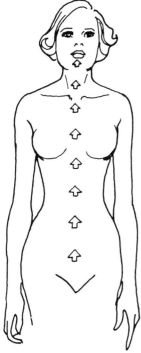

This is a very simple exercise. It stimulates the energy in the central meridan, and it is this energy flow that is associated with the brain. Test for a strong indicator muscle.
Run the hand from the pubic bone up the mid line to the middle of the bottom lip. This can be done six to ten times. Retest for a strong muscle response.
If you have a switched off response, run your hand up and down this central meridian from the pubic area to the bottom lip several times, finishing with several upward strokes.

Retest. If your muscle is still switched off do the Cook's Technique as described below.

2. Cook's Technique

This is the most effective Tibetan figure of 8 technique for switching on and is very useful in cases of over-energy.*

---

*Energy forms a figure 8 pattern on the front and back of the body. See *Acupuncture and body Energies* by W.A. McCarey.

Indications of over-energy are:
1. hyperactivity.
2. in testing the central meridian with the zipper exercise the results are reversed, i.e. if we run the central meridian from the pubic bone to the bottom lip and test, there would be a switched off response and when we run the meridian backwards, that is, from the bottom lip to the pubic bone, there would be a switched on response.

The *Cook's Technique* is divided into two parts.

1. First, be seated with the bottom into the back of the seat and with the chin in the air (do not drop into a slump posture).

Sitting in an upright position with both feet flat on the floor, take the left leg and place it over the right knee so that the ankle rests on the top of the knee of the right leg.

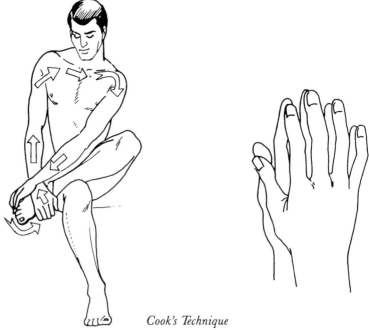

Cook's Technique

Figure 1

Figure 2

After doing that, take the right hand and place it across the left foot, across the area where the shoe laces would be on a shoe. Place the left forearm over the top of the right forearm so that the two arms are forming a cross just above the wrist. The left hand then curls around underneath the sole of the foot so that the fingertips are touching. (See Figure 1.) Take a deep breath and expel, relaxing the shoulders but maintaining this figure eight position. This position is then held for approximately one minute. Relax.

2. Sit squarely and uprightly on the chair and place both hands together so that the tips of *all* fingers touch. Press the tongue against the roof of the mouth. Hold this position for one minute. Remember to remain relaxed. (This position has the 'hands in prayer' appearance — see Figure 2.)

The Cook's Technique is very useful not only for correcting over-energy; it can be used when somebody has tested strongly on the two parallel lines or switched off on the cross or when the person is asked to cross crawl march and automatically starts with homolateral marching. At times it will also switch on the eyes when there is inhibition of ocular perception, that is, when the messages going from the eye to the brain are becoming confused; for auricular inhibition or difficulty perceiving auditory messages; and for co-ordinating physical movement.

Remember that although the Cook's Technique is one of seeming simplicity and one might question how it can make a difference, it is probably one of the most vital techniques in the range of procedures incorporated in the EK techniques.

The Cook's Technique can be a tremendous adjunct by clearing the blocks in and out of the brain so that the person is able to receive the instructions for the laterality repatterning and also allow him improved physical gross motor co-ordination, resulting in the ability to repattern. (See 'Laterality Repatterning').

The Cook's Technique is simple. It may not have a logical

32

or scientific reason for working, but it is tremendously effective. Do use it and value its application.

3. Brain Triangle

The third technique is the 'brain triangle' — a technique taken from acupressure for switching on or reducing message confusion.

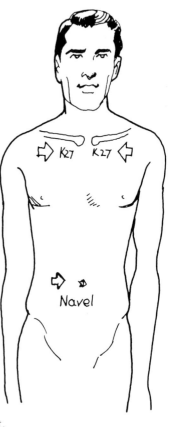

This is done by taking one hand and placing it over the naval. Little pressure is required. Take the index finger and the thumb of the other hand and place them on the bumps of the collar bone nearest the chest bone (see illustration), and then slide the finger and the thumb down off the bumps until they drop into the first depression. Once in that position vigorously rub these depressions for approximately 15 to 20 seconds while keeping the hand on the navel still.

Breathe normally throughout.

4. Cross Pattern Marching

Left arm, right leg, simultaneously.
Right arm, left leg simultaneously.

The person cross pattern marches slowly for 20 to 30 seconds. Test muscle. We are looking for a switched on muscle response. If a person has difficulty cross pattern marching place stickers of the same colour on knee and opposite arm so that he brings up the same coloured stickers simultaneously. Further, have him imagine that string is tied to one foot and to the opposite arm so that the two must come up together. You only need one piece of string between one arm and the opposite leg otherwise, as Phillip Crockford says, you may 'get your wires crossed'.

Now, homolaterally pattern, i.e. right arm/right leg simultaneously; left arm/left leg simultaneously for 20 to 30 seconds. Retest.

Cross pattern marching

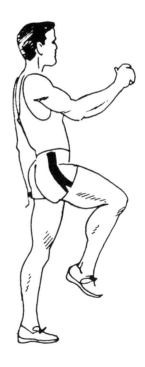

Homolateral marching

If the application of the intervention techniques has been successful, we should now have a switched on response on cross pattern marching and a switched off response on homolateral marching. Now test the X and ll.

This time we are looking for a strong response on the X and a switched off response on the parallel lines. Finally, to evaluate the change that may have taken place, have the person read forward. Evaluate the reading, comparing with before. Retest the muscle to establish whether you have a switched on or a switched off response. Reading forward may now produce a switched on response.

Have the person then read backwards again and note the difference. On completion of reading the paragraph backwards, retest and you may have a switching off response. The reason is that if those techniques integrate the two halves of the brain there will be less stress on reading forward, less stress on looking at the cross and less stress on cross pattern marching. All of which are integrated activities.

By bringing about an integration of the two halves of the brain, some of the observable changes will be:

1. Improved memory, particularly the short term memory, thus leading to improved comprehension.
2. Increase in concentration because there is less stress.
3. The eyes will cross the midline of the visual field more effectively.

Remember: Breathe normally throughout.

How long do the effects of these exercises last?

The benefits of the exercise may last for five minutes, for five days, or it may last forever. But the more often we use them, the less often we have to use them.

Development and Posture

When you were a baby, did you . . . ?
- 'Crawl' along by sitting on your bottom and not on all fours?
- Crawl for only a very short time?
- Crawl homolaterally? (See Figure 3.)

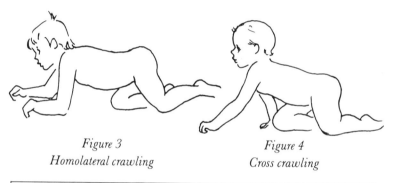

Figure 3
Homolateral crawling

Figure 4
Cross crawling

Do you, as a grown person, . . .?
- Constantly trip and fall over your own feet?
- Become irritable through frustration?
- Find yourself able to sit still for only a very short time?

Crawling

Nature provides the best opportunity for babies to integrate; and this is done over four stages.*

---

*These stages were identified by and are analysed in detail by Carl Delacarto *A new Start for the Child with Reading Problems*. Margaret Sassé, *Toddler Kindy Gymbaroo* stimulates the nervous system through movement and asks why we wait until a child is of school age before recognising its problems.

1. When the baby is in his cot, he raises his head and looks about. This enables him to cross the mid-visual field, transferring information to his brain more and more effectively as his ability to focus increases (at about six weeks).

2. As the baby starts to crawl, he raises one side of his body and keeps the other side to the mattress or floor. His head, ear and eye of that side are also to the floor, allowing development of the raised side. This procedure is then reversed as he raises the other side from the cot.

3. The baby then crawls along allowing left arm/right leg action and right arm/left leg action to occur. This action requires both sides of the brain to integrate and work together. When this stage is shortened either because the baby is an early walker or because walkers and playpens have been used, babies may develop learning difficulties. When the baby learns to stand, his ability to perceive visually and auditorially in space is enhanced as he uses both ears and eyes together.

4. Between four and seven years of age he develops laterality, i.e. becomes right handed, footed, eyed or left handed, footed, eyed.

Do you . . . ?
- **Slouch as you walk — finding it difficult to hold your head upright and 'walk tall'?**
- **Find it difficult to smile?**
- **Carry a handbag, case or parcels regularly on the one side?**
- **Have one shoulder higher than the other?**
- **Always cross the same leg over the other when you sit?**

Walking

The natural extension of the crawling step in later child-hood, adolescence and adulthood, is walking. As a person walks with the left foot/right arm and right foot/left arm movement, so, of course, he brings into action the left and the right brain. Again, by walking with the hands free, raising the eyes and looking to the left and right, the person's eyes cross the midline and integrate the left and the right hemispheres.

Today, when we walk, we often carry a handbag or books, which reduces the degree of integration. Again, jogging and running are marvellous for the physical integration of the left and the right brain as long as we look ahead and up rather than at our feet (which may be the switching down position).

The importance of posture

The importance of posture cannot be stressed enough.

Test A

Before starting:

1. Test for a switched on indicator muscle such as the deltoid.
2. Have the person sit comfortably in a chair. Test.

If you have discovered that, on sitting down, the person is switched off, have the person sit so that his bottom goes into the back of the chair and the chin is upright. (See Figure 5.) Retest. The muscle will test switched on again.

Now have the person move his bottom forward in the seat so that he becomes slightly slumped and dropped in the abdominal area. This will automatically throw the head forward in relation to the spinal column. (See Figure 6.) Retest. In most cases you will find that the slumped posture will cause the indicator muscle to switch off.

This simple test indicates the importance of good posture. For a muscle to lock into place, information has to pass backward and forward through the body and to the brain. When we slump, that line of communication from the body into the brain and back out into the muscle is impeded because the energy flow through the body is impeded. When we slump, we deny the internal organs the space they require to function. Moreover, when the head comes forward, the amount of room in the neck for the nerve supply to function fully is diminished.*

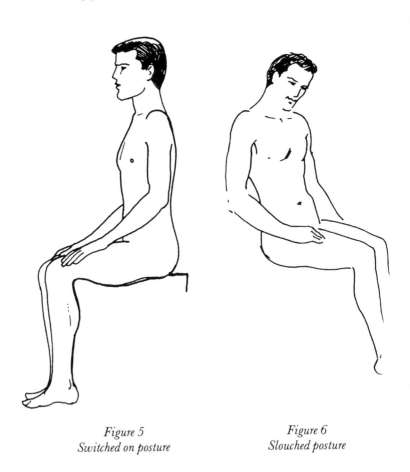

Figure 5
Switched on posture

Figure 6
Slouched posture

The Alexander Technique by Sarah Barker (Bantam, 1981) has some excellent advice on posture.

Test B

Another way of testing the importance of posture is to have somebody sit in an upright position, hold material to be read directly in front of his eyes and have him read the material. Retest the indicator muscle. In most situations the response will be switched on and the reading will be of an optimum standard irrespective of the reader's starting level of reading.

Now, drop the posture and assume a slumped position or another position (such as crossed legs) that may impede the transfer of the information in and out of the nervous system. Then place the reading material down in front towards the lap, have the person reread. In many instances, the standard of reading will diminish. By the same token, a muscle will be switched off, indicating that the slump posture again is switching off the channels that are available for messages to pass through the nervous system, causing a breakdown in the energy that flows through the body into the brain and back into the body. Look at people walking down the street — notice how many are walking along smiling, happy with life, and walking with a spring in their step. Unfortunately, we see very few who walk youthfully. Yet, when we do walk this way, we feel energetic *and* we feel happier. Imagine slumping the shoulders, dragging our feet *and* trying to look happy.

Practise standing and walking upright with the neck stretched slightly upwards. *Smile.* A smile is marvellous for switching on the system. It takes almost twice as many muscles to frown as it does to smile.

40

The Thymus

The thymus gland is located in the middle of the chest just beneath the upper part of the breast bone and is present in all mammals.

Often by tapping the thymus 15 to 20 times you will switch on your system. In the past the thymus gland was thought to be inactive. But Dr John Diamond recognised that this gland is in someway associated with the immune system.* When the thymus gland is removed or destroyed, the immune mechanisms and T. cells that guard the body against infection are less effective.

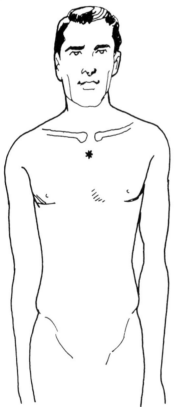

Exercise to check co-ordination
Rapidly tap the thymus gland using *both* hands alternatively. If this movement is not easily co-ordinated use the switching on techniques such as Cook's Technique, Brain Triangle, Cross Crawl Marching, and Laterality Repatterning. Then have the person retap the thymus to establish the increase in co-ordination.

*Dr John Diamond *Your Body Doesn't Lie*, Harper & Row NYC 1979.

Improving Visual Perception

Do you . . .?
- Turn your head so that you look out of one eye?
- Prefer to study lying on the floor rather than sitting at a desk?
- Move your head back and forwards rather than move your eyes when reading?
- Fall asleep when reading?

The messages that are received in the left visual field are transferred into the right hemisphere of the brain and the messages that are received through the right eye are crossed over to the left brain. This is a very complex neurological process of fusion.

Ocular inhibition occurs when:

1. The information will either not cross over at the channels where it ought to cross; or
2. Where it does cross over, it is passed through and does not get into the appropriate part of the brain; or
3. The information does not cross over and therefore is delivered to the same side.

When ocular inhibition occurs, some degree of confusion will take place. Reversed images is a common symptom. For example, 'b' may be written as 'd' or 'p' instead of 'q'. This is a common feature of dyslexia.

Test 1

If a person reads material fluently yet immediately after reading has no recollection of what has been read, the information has not reached the part of the brain that processes the information accurately.

In this situation, the use of the *Brain Triangle* is often effective. The Brain Triangle includes the area in the first depression underneath the front of the collar bone that we can feel or palpate. Rub these two areas while holding the navel with the other hand. (See illustration and discussion of the 'Brain Triangle' on p.32).

Test 2

Take a strong indicator muscle then give a visual stimulus by holding your finger directly in front of the person's eyes. Move your fingers into the subject's left visual field.

It is important that the subject's head does not move. The only thing that moves will be his eyes as they track the finger.

1. Have the person look far left and retest (Figure 7).
2. Then move the finger into the right visual field and retest the muscle with the eyes looking at the finger (Figure 8). Again ensure the head is being held straight ahead.
3. Move the finger back into the middle of the visual field and move the finger up above the middle of the visual field. Retest with the eyes in the up position (Figure 9).
4. Having tested, bring the eyes back down to the centre of the middle visual field and then take the eyes down towards the floor (Figure 10).

During all four of these tests, it is vital that the head remains stationary.

Figure 7

Figure 8

Figure 9   *Figure 10*

Stimulation. When any of the four areas of the visual field·
test switched off stimulate the brain triangle.

Test 3
A further procedure that can be used when testing for
ocular inhibition is to take the eyes diagonally up to the
right, test muscle response, diagonally up to the left, test,
diagonally down to the right, test, and diagonally down to
the left, test. This then gives us eight different directions in
which we can test the eyes.

The eyes may very well perceive an accurate image while
the stimulus is directly in front of the eyes, but when the
eyes move out of the centre of the visual field, there may be
difficulty.

Test 4
Ocular inhibition is indicated if the head rather than the
eyes tracks backward and forward as a person reads. This
is the body's defence mechanism. The head tracks backward and forward rather than take the eyes out of the
centre of the visual field into an extreme left or right position, where the eyes may experience stress.

Stimulation. Any, or all of these switching off processes may
be corrected by using the Brain Triangle or the Cook's
Technique, or by cross pattern marching without switching off, followed by cross pattern marching with the eyes
moving backwards and forwards across the visual field

from right to left. Having completed that, have the person continue marching while moving the eyes up and down from the roof to the floor and into the corners of the visual field, up and down diagonally to the right and to the left.

It is very rare for all of these techniques to be needed. You will usually find that one will correct all ocular inhibition problems.

Emotional stress factors and ocular inhibition
Somebody with a particular reading problem may find it extremely stressful to read in front of a group of people because of his past experiences.

In this case, the techniques already outlined for switching on or rectifying visual inhibition may be only temporarily effective and you would need to use the emotional stress release points.

First test for a switched on indicator muscle.

Have the person sit down and have him look at a book but not read it. Alternatively, have him close his eyes and visualise that he is standing and reading in front of a group of people.

Illustration indicating position of emotional stress release points.

While doing that, stand behind the person and place the pads of your finger tips on the emotional stress release points or frontal eminences. The frontal eminences are the most prominent bumps on the forehead directly above the pupil and are located between the eyebrows and the hair-line. The pressure on those points is only light. If you touch the points and then move your fingers an eighth of an inch to the side so that you feel your fingers pulling on the skin — that is sufficient pressure.

Hold those points lightly for one to two minutes and have the person visualise reading in front of a group. Once he has spent approximately one minute doing that, have him imagine himself continuing reading but seeing himself doing it confidently and without any stress involved.

After two minutes, release the points.

Having completed this, have the person read a passage aloud and observe any change in the fluency of the reading. Note changes in the tone of the voice. Retest. The muscle should test stronger — you may have to repeat this procedure a few times to remove the stress the person feels; but the more it is done, the less you have to do it.

The Dominant Eye

Each person has a dominant eye, that is the eye that leads the vision.

How to determine the dominant eye
1. Tear a hole in the middle of a piece of paper and hold it up with both hands at arm's length.
2. Focus on an object through the hole with *both* eyes open.
3. Bring the paper to the face, keeping the object in sight.
4. The hole will come to the dominant eye.

Further test
Follow steps 1 and 2 but this time cover one eye at a time. When you cover the dominant eye the object will disappear from view.

The dominant eye and handwriting*

People who have poor handwriting can generally improve it by moving the page they are writing on so that it is more in line with the dominant eye. As they write left to right across the page, the free hand keeps the page moving so it is always in front of the dominant eye. Muscle test page positions to find the optimum writing position.

Writing is often enhanced by writing on a slope board or sloped desk. Writing at a slope board also keeps the spine straight — the head is held at the best position for energy flow with the eyes looking straight ahead. (A Balens chair may also be valuable.)

Take up your writing position at the slope desk. Put the pen to the page and muscle test. If you have poor handwriting despite all other tests having had a switched on response, you may find this slope board will solve your untidy handwriting.

Many people find a slope of approximately 20 degrees is satisfactory and permits greatly improved writing.

Moving a person's books or position in the classroom to be more in line with the dominant eye should be done once laterality has been established. A temporary change of position may possibly ease the work while laterality is being established. The need for the person being on the correct side of the room is less important once he has been switched on.

Back Tracking

It is very important in early childhood development, when the pathways or the crossing over of the messages in and out of the brain are being established, for a person to spend sufficient time lying prone (on his tummy). This allows the

---

*For further information, see the section 'Horizontal Eights — up and out', p. 50. Paul Dennison's *Switching On* is also recommended. We understand that the English Teachers Association of Australia has published a book dealing with the relationship between the brain and handwriting but have no details of it.

eyes to learn a full range of movement while observing the world around him. If this is not done in those early developmental years, the neurological development may be impaired and the switching over of the information is slowed down or impeded.

But it is never too late to develop those patternings, or crossing over of information, and one of the ways this is done is by *Back Tracking*.

As adults, we don't necessarily need to lie down on our abdomen and look up at the world with the head tilted backwards. What we can do is sit upright in a chair, tilt the head backwards, and look at the ceiling. Then raise one arm vertically so that the fingers are seen directly above the face. (See Figure 11, p. 48.)

The head must be stationary and, when we start moving the hand (which is the visual stimulus), the head must not move with it. It is important that the movement is performed with the eyes and not with the head. Move the arms slowly through an arc from left to right and closely watch the finger at all times.

This exercise is a valuable one but one that should follow all other forms of ocular inhibition exercises. Although it is very effective and can correct problems with the eyes crossing the midline, if the ocular inhibition is substantial and we have not corrected that first, then this will be a very stressful and difficult exercise to perform.

Indications that the exercise is a stressful one are: discolouration of the face (the face starts to become red); the eyes start to leap instead of smoothly tracking backward and forward or the head starts moving; or the head may cease to be held in the backward position and may move into an upright position.

Note:
1. It is important to remember that this exercise is not used in the early stages of intervention. This technique would be used in the third or fourth EK session when

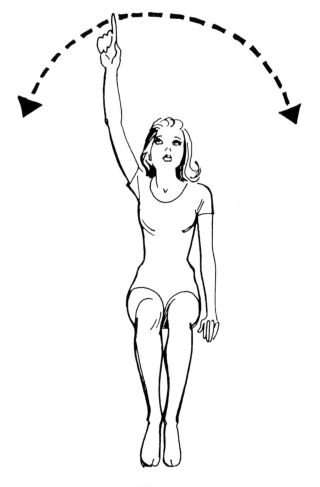

Figure 11

switching on has been established and is starting to be maintained at an optimum level.

2. If correcting ocular inhibition and using the back tracking exercise on a regular basis causes stress and/or a weak muscle response, discontinue. Cervical sublux-ation may be present, i.e. one of the seven small bones in the neck area may be misaligned. If this is the case, it

is important to seek the advice of a practitioner in the chiropractic or osteopathic field to have that problem assessed and corrected. The switching off that occurs is the body's defence mechanism to prevent it from becoming overstressed. If subluxation of the spine remains unattended the corrections made using EK techniques will often be temporary.

Case Study

John's reading was average but not as good as he would have liked. Using the Zipper, Brain Triangle and Laterality Repatterning, we were able to improve his reading.

His handwriting was difficult to read so we muscle tested to find the best position for the paper; we then had him write on a 20 degree slope board, which further improved his writing.

John kept tilting his head so we stimulated the brain triangle. This corrected a slight ocular inhibition but the tilt remained. When he held his head straight, his reading deteriorated. To improve his reading he tilted his head. A switched off response to muscle testing indicated misalignment of the temporomandibular joint so chiropractic help was suggested. But, as a final correction before John left, we sat him in the Cook's position. The results were dramatic — every test was now switched off and his reading deteriorated!

We re-established the Zipper to being switched on, and the chiropractor corrected the temporomandibular joint misalignment and neck subluxation. At his next appointment, John tested switched on on everything and read very well. He maintains this switched on state.

Horizontal Eights
— up and out

The benefits
This exercise has a number of benefits. It is an .exercise that will improve handwriting and it will enhance the eye's ability to cross the centre of the visual field and fuse vision in the middle of the visual field. It may increase both memory and concentration.

It is particularly indicated when somebody has a 'blind spot' in his visual field, meaning that in one particular area of the visual field, the eyes do not convey the message accurately to the brain. This is automatically indicated by:

1. Spelling the beginning and the end of words accurately yet constantly making mistakes in the centre of the word.
2. Reading effectively and fluently at the beginning and the end of the sentence but ignoring the middle.

These problems occur because the crossing over mechanism that allows the eyes to fuse the two images they receive into a single vision, rather than double or distorted one, has a block in it. It is either switched off or some distortion or disorganisation of the messages is occurring.

The exercise
In doing this exercise, it is important that the person sits upright in the chair facing the desk or the table squarely and not distort the body posture at all.

It is often a good idea to tape the page or the book to the table.

Start in the exact middle of the page and draw figures of eight horizontally on the page, moving up and outwards one over the top of the other.

One of the techniques used with a child when doing this exercise is to have him pretend that his pen is a car and he is actually driving the car around the race track. The movement needs to be done as spontaneously and fluently as possible.

Points to watch

The most important point about horizontal eights is to remember that the eight must start in the middle and go up and out. It doesn't matter whether it goes up and out to the

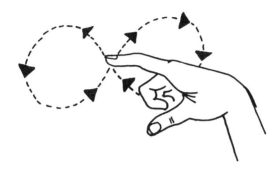

left or up and out to the right but it must go up and out rather than down and in. This is because the action of going up and out is the basic or elementary fine motor skill that is required when writing the English language in script form. To write the English language effectively in running or script writing, we need to form circles primarily in an anti-clockwise direction. Once we have formed the letters, we can then connect to the next letter and move across the page to the right as we write.

If this action becomes stressful for the person performing it, it is often an indication that he has a preference for operating more strongly out of one eye than the other. In this case, the body may start to distort into a tilted posture, or the head start to tilt to one side, allowing the vision to be seen by one eye dominantly. Correct this by using the Brain Triangle (see p. 32).

Once fusion is restored, the horizontal eight becomes easier to do and, when the eyes are switched on, the eights will reinforce that switching on.

In many cases of *severe handwriting difficulties* the activity of holding on to the pen and doing a small figure of eight on the desk may be very difficult and stressful. The person will probably reverse the direction of the racetrack, moving down and in instead of up and out. To overcome this, have him use a very large pen, or even take a large cylinder and strap the pen to the cylinder, or have him clench the fist and tape the pen to the fist. The activity then becomes a gross motor action, using the arm, rather than a fine motor action using the hands and fingers.

To make it even simpler, use either a white board, butchers' paper on a wall, or a chalk board so that the eights can be done as large figures rather than as small fine-detailed figures. This again incorporates a gross motor rather than fine motor action and, in most cases, is less stressful than the fine motor skill.

By doing this exercise regularly, writing can improve, holding the pen correctly can be established, and finer detail and control can be brought about. Slowly reduce the size of the eight and the writing implement until it is a pen. The first time the pen is included in the activity, tape the pen to the back of the index finger and have the person do the eight. This will instil confidence in the learner in creating the action by himself, thus diminishing the amount of stress he experiences in his hand.

One of the advantages of using either a chalk board or a white board is that there is less permanency about what is done. It is much easier to remove the image and start again. There is less stress on the learner to get it right the first time. The less the stress the better the work.

What to do in difficult cases
When writing is very stressful for the learner we should break the process down into simpler steps so that the

learner can constantly achieve success. To do this, take the writing instrument away and have him draw the eights with his finger in the air. This takes away the stress of producing an end result but teaches and reinforces the motor skill of doing the figure of eight.

Again, when drawing the horizontal eight in the air, on a white board, or on a small piece of paper, it is essential that the horizontal eights are drawn directly in front of the person as he faces straight ahead so that the cross over of the eight occurs exactly in the middle of the visual field. This gives the maximum visual integration.

Horizontal Eight tables

The person who has difficulty co-ordinating fine or gross motor skills, yet handles number sequencing well, could well learn to do the horizontal eight if the horizontal eight is placed on paper as in the figure below.

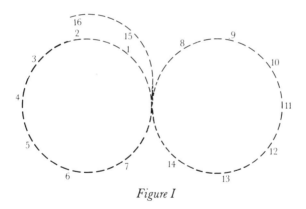

Figure I

Rather than draw an eight on the page, write numbers from one upwards in the direction of the eight (Figure I). Now have the student join the numbers together (Figure II). In doing so the student will 'draw' an eight. So start in the middle with '1' and then an inch away put '2' and then another inch away put '3' and then another inch away put

'4'; keep going around to form an eight. Start the next number around the original eight again, continually increasing the size of the eight so that we are actually working at a number level rather than at a motor level (Figure III). This will often overcome problems where people are unable to co-ordinate the activity.

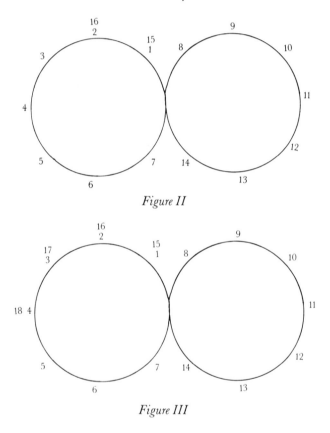

Figure II

Figure III

This exercise develops many different functions:
1. It integrates the two halves of the brain.
2. It integrates the eyes and fuses the vision in the middle of the visual field.
3. It improves fine and gross motor co-ordination skills.

4. It is a method for learning tables and counting.
5. It is a method for learning the alphabet.

To learn multiplication tables

Start by numbering around the figure of eight from one to twelve, the '1' starting in the centre and the '12' finishing in the centre with the numbers equally spaced throughout.

Then, place numbers around the figure of eight in denominations of two, so that where you have '1' you would put '2', where you have '2' you would put '4', where you have '3' you would put '6', '4' would be '8', '5' would be '10' and you

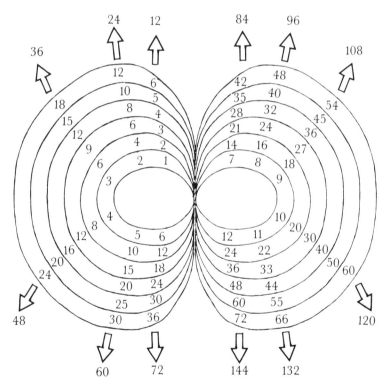

continue that around the eight until you finish back in the middle at '12' and you have 12 and 24 to complete.

Then, next to the '2' place '3' and continue around the figure of eight in denominations of three until you get to the middle again and the number '36'. Start again at number '1', this time placing '4' at the top and going around 4, 8, 12, 16 and so on through to 48.

If, for instance, we want to work out what 2 x 5 is, look at the middle of the horizontal eight. Move to the second row to No. 2 — follow the horizontal eight around to where 5 occurs on the first row. Look at the second row again — the answer to 2 x 5 = 10.

This will assist those who have difficulty with linear or sequential processing. Counting may also be substituted.

Horizontal Eight alphabet

This same exercise may be used substituting the alphabet for numbers, facilitating the learning of the alphabet at the same time as doing an integration exercise.

If we look at the horizontal eight and draw a line down through the centre we can place the letters of the alphabet in the appropriate hemisphere.

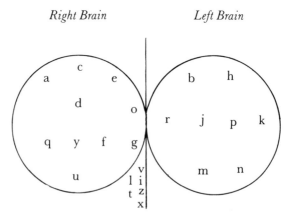

Right brain — all circles are formed counterclockwise and there is a circle before the stroke.

Left brain — all letters have the stroke before the circle and the circle is formed in a clockwise direction.

If there is a difficulty with the information being conveyed into the appropriate hemisphere then it is logical that the person will see 'b's as 'd's. Where there is confusion more people substitute 'b' for 'd' than 'd' for 'b'. A correction for this is to have the learner hold a pen in both hands while you face him and clasp his hands in your own.

Using a gross motor action and bending the knees, both of you draw the letter with the hands. For example draw the letter 'd' and, as you move your arms to form a huge 'd' say aloud 'around, up and down'. Much success has been achieved with this method by teaching all the left brain letters first and then all the right brain letters.

Body Eights or Jolly Jumbos

Do you . . . ?
- Find it easy to say what you think but find it difficult to express yourself in writing?
- Find it difficult to stretch your hands out in front of you and then bring them together so that your fingertips meet easily?
- Mix up your left and right hands?
- Experience neck tension when reading and writing?
- Have poor memory?
- Have poor concentration?

Whole Body Eights are indicated to enhance memory, speaking and listening skills.

Method
1. Stand.
2. Bend knees.
3. Push bottom out.
4. Keep the head straight and raise either arm to touch the ear while pointing to the ceiling. Note — keep the head straight, bring the arm to the ear not the ear to the arm.
5. Using the whole body and with the eyes looking towards your fingertips, move the body to form an eight. Use as much space and body movement as you can. Keep the action fluent and cross the midline directly in front of you, bending at the knees to reduce possible strain on the lower back. Repeat using other arm; then both arms together.

In the process of releasing stress or tension of muscles, short term discomfort or pain may be experienced. It is advisable to stop even though this discomfort is only temporary and to do the exercise more frequently for short periods only.

Body eights or Jolly Jumbos are used to enhance your memory — when you are studying combine this exercise with right brain processes such as the use of memories, colourful patterns, shapes or diagrams and use your imagination to make your work more realistic and colourful and therefore more easily remembered.

Improving Auditory Perception

Do you . . . ?
• Fall asleep watching TV?
• Forget names easily?
• Mix up telephone numbers?

Stress deafness occurs when information coming in via the ears is not properly transmitted or processed along the channels for clear recall or understanding of the information.

Somebody who switches off with auditory messages will confuse the spoken message, confuse or reverse telephone numbers, forget names, and may have difficulty verbalising information he has received previously or when taking dictation.

Method 1

Have the person stand and test the supraspinatus (fig leaf) muscle for a strong response. Having established a strong response, have the person turn his head to the left so that his right ear is the one nearest to you as you stand in front of him. Tell the person to 'hold' his arm as you muscle test, so that the message is received primarily through the right ear. Immediately test the muscle.

If auditory inhibition is present, the muscle response will be switched off.

Now, turn the head to the right, so that the left ear is nearest to the person speaking. Tell him to 'hold' so that the message is received primarily into the left ear and retest the muscle. Again, if inhibition occurs, the muscle response will switch off.

Method 2

Have the person stand and look straight ahead. With one hand cover the right ear so that the verbal message given is received primarily in the left ear. Muscle test.

Then, taking the hand from the right ear, place it over the left ear so that the message delivered is received in the right ear. Muscle test again.

What to do with a switched off response

Should either or both ears indicate switching off, there are two ways to correct this.

The first is to take the outer portion of the ear and roll the curve of the ear outwards. This is done an equal number of times on both ears for about 20 seconds, rolling the entire peripheral of the ear out and back. Retest, using the same testing procedure as before. The muscle response will now be switched on. The ear has associated points of all of the body's major reflex areas in microcosm so unrolling the ear is often a very effective method of switching on the system.

The second method of overcoming auricular inhibition or auditory switching is to place one hand over the navel and the other hand on the mastoid process or bump on the back of the skull, just under and behind the ear (see diagram). Do this with each ear for approximately 15-20 seconds. Retest for a switched on response.

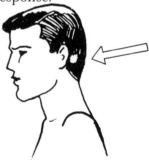

Laterality

To perform a task with optimum ease and efficiency one brain and its associated hand, ear, eye and foot must be dominant and the other brain must be subordinate. When one half of the brain is working, the other half is either relaxing or performing tasks that do not require conscious control.

A person with a *dominant left brain* will optimally be:

> right handed
> right eyed
> right eared
> right footed.

A person with a *dominant right brain* will optimally be:

> left handed
> left eyed
> left eared
> left footed.

Most people fall into one category or the other. When the pattern is consistent and complete sidedness apparent the two halves of the brain co-operate to work efficiently and learning difficulties are minimised.

Mixed dominance

We have found that some people show mixed laterality. For example, the left eye may be dominant but they may be right handed and/or left footed.

Optimally, a person has his laterality associated with his dominant brain (but this is not always so). After Laterality Repatterning and Cook's Technique we have often found that the laterality is no longer mixed but is completely one sided. This is probably because the earlier testing may not have been able to gain a clear and accurate picture of the dominance and so may have indicated mixed dominance rather than that the actual dominance had changed.

Dr P. Dennison points out that when the pattern is inconsistent or mixed, the two brains are more likely to become confused over their work and energy is drained from the system.

Since reading, writing and spelling are integrated processes generally involving a left brain orientation, the ideal pattern would be for a person to be left brained and right handed, right eyed, right eared and right footed. Such a person's left brain analyses facts while his right brain subconsciously processes word recognition, writing movement and listens to the rhythm of the words, organising the parts into a whole.*

Case Study

Bob was a very bright sales executive with a very specific problem. His writing was very neat and his memory and concentration sharp. But his oral reading was poor, being slow, very broken and monosyllabic.

He tested switched on when he looked at the parallel lines (II), when he read backwards or when he thought about reading to himself. However, he tested switched off when he looked at the cross (X), when he read forwards, when he thought about reading aloud, and when he was tested for visual perception and backtracking.

But, after doing the Brain Buttons exercise he tested switched on for visual perception and backtracking, and after Laterality Repatterning he tested switched on for X and reading forwards, and switched off for II and reading backwards.

---

*For those interested in a detailed study of split brain and block dominant function see *Left Brain — Right Brain* by Skinner and Deutsch.

When his oral reading was reassessed after these exercises, Bob's improvement was the greatest we have ever witnessed in one session. Bob was obviously shocked and could not believe so dramatic an improvement could take place in so short a time. He told us about the enormous stress and embarrassment his poor oral reading had caused him and that it had hindered his professional progress.

At this stage we had had only two sessions together. He then pursued emotional stress release techniques and his reading improved still further. He is now national sales manager of his company.

Laterality Repatterning

Perhaps the most important, the most significant, or the most effective EK technique is Laterality Repatterning.

Laterality Repatterning means taking the body and the brain through a reprogramming technique. Somebody has a learning difficulty because information is not getting through to that part of the brain which processes and allows accurate intake, recall and expression of that information. This happens for a variety of reasons, some of which we have already discussed, but all come under the general heading of stress.

We experience stress in four ways: *chemical, structural, environmental* and *emotional*.

Any or all of these components of stress can be present and be the reason for switching off.

In Laterality Repatterning we are giving information to the brain to allow it to repattern so that what was previously a stressful stimulus is no longer stressful for it, thus allowing both halves of the brain to become integrated and able to communicate easily to each other.

The three steps to achieve Laterality Repatterning

Step One. Stimulate the activity of the left half of the brain or the 'try' brain as Dr Dennison calls it. The person homo-laterally marches, i.e. with the right leg and right arm simultaneously and the left leg and the left arm simultaneously with the head facing straight ahead, *move the eyes down into the right visual field* (see Figures 12 and 13). The purpose of this is to activate the left hemisphere while giving it two tasks to perform at the same time.

You will recall that the left half of the brain likes to do things in a very sequential, step-by-step manner and it doesn't like to do simultaneous tasks such as homolateral marching on the spot and looking down into the right hand corner (both of which activates the left half of the brain). Therefore, what we are doing in this first stage is programming into the brain that the left hemisphere works *less effectively on its own* and is stressed by simultaneous tasks (such as are required if it were reading or writing).

Test the muscle — the response should be switched off.

Figure 12
Homolateral marching

Figure 13
Eyes down to right visual field

Step Two. Initiate the use of the right hemisphere of the brain — the side which likes to do simultaneous activities, synthesising and putting the pieces together into a whole.

The person cross pattern marches, i.e. the left leg and the right arm work simultaneously and the right arm and left leg work simultaneously during which times the eyes look up into the left visual field (see Figures 14 and 15). Cross pattern marching involves both sides of the brain and, by looking up to the left while marching, we are activating the right hemisphere as well as stimulating its activity.

Each of these activities should be performed for approximately two minutes.

Test the muscle — the response will be switched on.

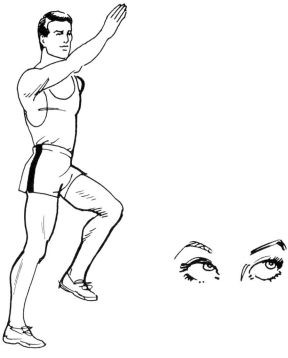

Figure 14
Cross pattern marching

Figure 15
Eyes up to left visual field

Step Three. Program or anchor the information into the brain.

When performing these steps the person testing the muscle response should stand behind so as not to distract the subject's visual attention from his hands.

Have the person stand up and look straight ahead with both arms outstretched to the sides with the palms facing upwards. Then have the person imagine that in his left hand he holds the right hemisphere of the brain, and in his right hand he holds the left hemisphere of the brain. We then verbalise some of the characteristics of the two halves of the brain. 'In your left hand you have the right hemisphere of your brain which likes to take all the pieces and put them together to form a whole. It is the one that likes to do things in a gestalt or a whole manner. In the opposite, in your right hand, imagine that you are holding the left hemisphere of your brain and that's the part of the brain that processes information in a very logical, one-at-a-time sequence. Imagine that you can feel them in your hands. How much do they weigh? What do they feel like? What temperature are they? Now, slowly bring your hands from the outside, with your fingers spread out, in toward the centre where they will join.'

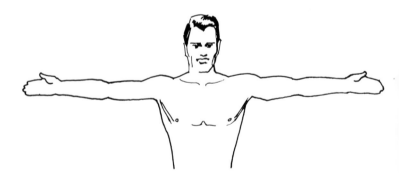

Once the hands start to move in towards the centre and you can see both hands clearly, focus on the hands and watch them as they slowly come together. Have the fingers open so that when near to contact, the fingers can interlock to form a whole.

Once they have completely joined, clench the two hands together in an integrated mass and feel them combined into one unit. Hold them relaxed in front of you in that position and take a very deep breath, letting the breath out as you relax and allow the hands to break and drop by the side.

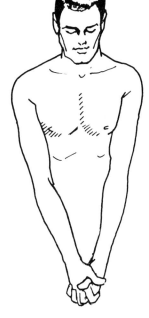

Note

Perform this activity with the tester who is doing the talking standing behind the person carrying out the laterality repatterning. The tester should use the words exactly as they appear above so all the possible methods of processing information are initiated. We are giving the person auditory, visual and kinesthetic (related to feeling and touch) cues. We are giving him an opportunity to feel how heavy the brain is, to feel the fingers coming together in an integrated mass. We are seeing the integration occur and we are hearing about how the two halves blend together to form a whole.

Laterality Repatterning is a complex activity and each of the steps requires a high level of neurological activity. Therefore, a person who is severely switched off and is having severe learning difficulties, particularly those who have gross motor co-ordination problems, will find this a very difficult activity to perform.

In this instance, we suggest one of two things.

1. Work with the previous switching on exercises, particularly the Cook's Technique until such time as gross motor co-ordination becomes an easier activity for the person to perform.

2. The person being tested could lie down to perform the laterality repatterning. Give him *one* task to perform, such as keeping his eyes down in the right visual field, while you physically move his limbs for him. During this time it is important that the head stays in the neutral position, facing straight ahead.

This will assist anyone who has co-ordination difficulties and finds it difficult to integrate all activities simultaneously.

Severe learning difficulty

When someone has severe learning difficulties do *not* use Laterality Repatterning in the early stages. It is very valuable for the person to experience many small successes. If he can see that he is improving in a number of areas, he will gain the confidence to tackle a more difficult task (such as Laterality Repatterning) at a later stage.

Transposed hemispheres

Very rarely does one encounter a person with transposed hemispheres. The left hemisphere, which normally processes information in a logical, sequential fashion, works as though it were the right hemisphere. Conversely, the right hemisphere, which usually operates in the holistic or simultaneously processing manner, acts as though it were the left hemisphere.

As mentioned above, the occasions when this occurs will be very rare, but two groups of people in which it is prevalent are the Japanese and Polynesian races because the Japanese and Polynesian languages tend to be vowel-oriented. This changes completely the sound of the languages and, therefore, in the early childhood developmental stages, these people quite often process information in a reverse fashion to people from other countries.

If a person has transposed hemispheres the Cook's Technique and Laterality Repatterning will produce a switched off response.

When doing Laterality Repatterning, we need to change the process of the eye movement so that when homolaterally marching, the person looks down to the left rather than down to the right and when cross pattern marching, he looks up to the right rather than up to the left.

When doing the Cook's Technique, reverse the process and put the right leg over the left leg, the left hand over the right foot and the right hand over the left hand and under the sole of the right foot.

By reversing these two processes, you will find that the response is now switched on.

After having completed all three steps, complete the process by having the person march on the spot and move the eyes back and forward, up and down through a complete range of movements in the visual field and retest for a switched on response.

How long does Laterality Repatterning last?

How long Laterality Repatterning lasts is a question that is often asked and a difficult one to answer. In the main, most people will find that when they do Laterality Repatterning in conjunction with other EK techniques they will remain switched on for a longer period of time than if the person did the EK exercises only. In severe cases this will not necessarily be the case, but the more often Laterality Repatterning is performed, the longer it will last, although the length of time will vary with the individual.

We usually suggest when working with somebody with moderate learning difficulties and with moderate co-ordination problems, that he perform Laterality Repatterning once a week for perhaps two or three months and then once a month thereafter.

In more severe cases, make it a daily activity for two or three weeks, then weekly, and then decrease over a period of time to perhaps once a month.

Case Study

Garry is 10 years of age, in 4th Class.
He does not like school.
He has a history of food sensitivities.
Had a difficult birth and was ill on and off for the first 3 years.

Learning Difficulties:

Writing
— Very poor and well below the standard of his age.
— He forms all circles clockwise.
— Has difficulty in the middle visual field.
— Had difficulty doing Horizontal Eights (up and out) and performed Horizontal Eights (down and in) with seeming ease.

Reading

— Slow, broken, and monosyllabic.
— He was 2 years below his reading age.
— He had little to no recall.
— He also became very tired when reading.

Tests

Switched On	*Switched Off*
— When tested with parallel lines	— When tested with the 'X'
— When tested on Horizontal Eights down and in)	— When tested on Horizontal Eights (up and out)
— Reading backwards	— When reading forward
— Printing	— When script writing
— When writing circles clockwise	— When tested for visual perception in all 4 directions
— Homolateral marching	— When tested for auditory perception, both left and right
	— When writing circles counter clockwise
	— When backtracking with eyes
	— When cross marching

First Visit

The only tests and exercises which produced a positive change were:

1. Brain triangle switched on his muscle response to the visual perception test (no change in reading).
2. Ear rolling switched on his auditory perception.

The exercises which produced no change were:
— Cook's Technique
— Horizontal Eights (up and out)
— backtracking
— cross marching

During Visits one and two he used only Brain Triangles, ear rolling and Cook's Technique.

Second Visit

His muscle response to all tests and exercises were positive after Repatterning which was no longer stressful to him. Both he and his mother acknowledged minor changes in his work. We added Horizontal Eights (up and out) and Repatterning to his exercise routine.

Third Visit

Garry was now testing positively on all tests.

As a result his performance had changed significantly in all areas originally assessed, including forming circles counter clockwise, forming Horizontal Eights (up and out). He was also able to remember and verbalise some of what he had read.

Garry continues to make progress.

Food Testing

Do you . . . ?
- Eat and then feel tired?
- Develop a rash after eating certain foods?
- Feel brighter after eating parsley or capsicum?
- Develop a headache after drinking tea or coffee?
- Are you hyperactive after eating?
- Are you irritable after eating?
- Do you crave certain foods?

In food testing, we are looking for two things:
1. Foods that create a switching off effect, i.e. those foods that, for some reason, cause a physical reaction in the body that prevents messages passing along the nervous system.
2. Those foods that cause a positive switching on response in the body and facilitate the passage of messages along the nervous system.

How we test for food responses
Muscle test the Penguin *(Latissimus Dorsi)*, which is associated with the spleen, or the Flyer *(Pectoralis Major Clavicular)*, which is associated with the stomach. Having established a strong indicator muscle, take the particular food you wish to test and place it under the tongue or on the tongue. Retest the muscle.

The food will either cause a switching on effect and strengthen the muscle response or it will have no effect and the muscle will remain the same. It may even switch the muscle off.

Food is classified into three categories according to its effect on the body:

foods that switch us on — biogenic foods
foods that have no effect — biostatic foods
foods that switch us off — biocidic foods

Points to remember
The food being tested must only be put into the mouth and not be chewed or swallowed. Having tested and assessed the effect of the food, the food should then be removed from the mouth and the mouth rinsed out with water before testing another food.

It is preferable that this process be performed with only three foods at any one testing session. If done on a daily basis and the results charted, we may obtain an accurate overview of the body's ability to tolerate specific foods.

If a food tested on six different occasions produces three or more negative responses out of six, then the food should not be eaten for a minimum of three months. During this period the body should increase its immunity to that substance.

After the food has been eliminated for three months, it may be reintroduced to the diet. Observe any reactions in learning ability, behaviour or physical responses such as headaches, blurred vision or digestive disturbances. They may all be a result of food sensitivities.

Another example of an adverse response to food may be unusual fatigue. It should diminish if you abstain from the food causing the problem. If the body has not developed immunity to that food during the period of abstinence, then the reaction will reoccur when the food is introduced. Often the reaction will be worse than it was initially.

If this happens, it is most important that the food be removed from the diet for another period of three months. If the food, upon reintroduction, causes no adverse responses and does not cause a switching off effect when being muscle tested, then introduce the food into the diet on a once-a-week basis for a period of three months and then return to the diet as normal.

Foods that should be tested are high sugar foods, refined foods, foods with artificial colourings, flavourings or preservatives, chocolate and coffee. These are foods' that invariably trigger a switching off response in the body and are ideal for initial testing purposes to validate the effectiveness of the tests.

On the other hand, foods that usually produce a switched on effect are parsley and capsicum.

Often it is safe to say that foods with a life component such as a plant (parsley, seeds, nuts) will generally bring about a positive response and a switching on effect. Again test the individual — for some people grains and nuts will cause a food sensitivity reaction and a switching off effect. Food sensitivities are often transient things. At different times sensitivity will develop to different things. A person might eat a particular food substance for years and suddenly develop a sensitivity to it. On the other hand, the sensitivity to a particular food may just as quickly disappear. For this reason it is important to have a testing method, such as the EK food testing procedure, that is accurate, safe (since the food is not swallowed) and takes a matter of seconds to conduct.

Surrogate Testing

Case Study

George was born after a very stressful pregnancy and difficult birth as he was in the transverse lie position. After birth he gained tremendous comfort from a dummy and hated to be parted from it. He appeared placid until he walked. Occasionally he turned denim

blue which was diagnosed as cardio-vascular depriva-
tion and his mother was told he 'would grow out of it'.

At four months, when he was holding his head well,
he was placed in a car seat, which he hated. His
mother thought he squirmed with pain but doctors
could not find any reason other than 'he just hates
cars'.

He crawled for six weeks or so and then stood and
walked at nine months. He was extremely bow-legged
but X-rays indicated that nothing was wrong with his
hips.

George progressed normally but his parents' feelings that 'something was wrong' persisted. He would
not sit throughout meals and still hated car trips.
Despite being active, he was not hyperactive and his
parents felt that he was cranky at times as if 'frustrated
within himself'. He fell over fairly frequently and
always had bruises on his head.

At 17 months he and his family went on holiday
where he was able to take off long winter clothes. As
he ran down a slope he fell several times. Watching
him, his parents said that 'he had little or no observable rotation of his hips, his legs were bent in and his
left foot was pigeon-toed'. As he ran he tripped himself
on his turned-in foot.

His inability to talk, despite obvious comprehension of all things going on around him, or the fact that
he 'read' his books upside down, prompted his parents
to use EK with him at least twice each day and
whenever holding or cuddling him. All fourteen
meridians (see John Thie, *Touch for Health* for a
detailed study of the meridians of the body) were
tested and seven were found to be going the wrong
way. These meridians were flushed and run in the correct direction.

Because he walked homolaterally, his parents moved his left leg/right arm simultaneously for him and his right leg/left arm simultaneously for him as he lay down. This helped both halves of his brain to work together rather than have him use the left hemisphere predominantly as he had been doing. His brain triangle was stimulated several times daily.

At the time of writing his parents had been using EK techniques with George for five days. They commented that he was happier within himself, he was able to sit comfortably at a table without wanting to run about in the middle of a meal, and it seemed easier for him to walk. He fell over infrequently. Moreover, his legs appeared to be straightening and he bent his knees more easily. He now enjoyed car trips.

A programme has been established to improve his co-ordination and reflexes using EK techniques. Within two days of having his meridians flushed, he said three words and held his books up the right way when 'reading'.

Surrogate testing uses a substitute or another person to test babies, children, and those who find it difficult to hold their muscles in order to gain a clear reading, and those who are invalid and unable to be muscle tested.

1. Test the surrogate for a strong indicator muscle.
2. Have the surrogate touch the person being tested and the top of the head if convenient or otherwise the arm, shoulder or hand.
3. Test the surrogate. If the person being tested is switched off, the surrogate's muscle will now test switched off.

4. Do the exercises with the person being tested (not the surrogate).
5. Retest using the surrogate.

Surrogate testing is a very useful method of testing infants for food sensitivity.

Emotional Stress Release

Do you . . . ?
- Cry often?
- Have difficulty turning your head to either side?
- Suffer from headaches?
- Find it difficult to smile?
- Walk   faster than most people?
- Eat faster than most people?
- Feel pressured?
- Become angry at very small or insignificant things?

Case Study
Graham is fourteen years old. He tested switched on using the Zipper, Brain Triangle and when cross pattern marching, but switched off when reading. He had not smiled for two years and was unable to turn his head fully to one side.

We decided to use ESR to release the tension he felt about school and employment. After holding his ESR points for a few minutes, he began to speak quite freely about his fears. We maintained contact with the ESR points while he talked his worries through. After quite some time he relaxed and began chatting. Graham began to smile easily and found he could now turn his head fully to either side.

Emotional Stress Release (ESR)

One of the major challenges that we frequently encounter is that poor reading tends to be accompanied by emotional problems.

If poor reading is a result of psychological or emotional problems, why do children and adults who have a problem in reading not have problems in other subjects that do not require reading? Many children who do not read very well are very good at mental arithemtic and, of course, if their problems were psychological or emotional, it would appear that they should have difficulties with mental arithmetic as well as with reading and writing. It seems that the two are not related to the emotional problem but rather the emotional problem is a result of the reading problem.

One of the most commonly recognised factors involved in learning difficulties, and one of the hardest to overcome, is the effect of stress on the learner. There are four different categories of stress:

1. Chemical stress, brought about by certain foods and preservatives that we eat.

2. Emotional stress resulting from fear, grief, anger and frustration.
3. Structural stress resulting from a misaligned skeletal system, primarily the spinal column.

   Probably the most important single structural factor related to neurological disorganisation and hence learning difficulties is misalignment of the temporomandibular joint (TMJ). Misalignment of the TMJ or joints of the jaw is indicated by grinding of the teeth or a 'clicky' jaw. A further consideration is the muscle structure of the body which indicates it is stressed by being misaligned (one side of the body is stronger than the other). This is not necessarily related to handedness.
4. Environmental stress includes such things as music (rock music with a dum-dum-da beat), light (fluorescent as compared to incandescent light), colours, furniture, noise levels, air pollutants.

These four categories of stress are inter-related and, if one form of stress is present, then, in time, it will cause other types of stress to occur. For instance, if somebody were constantly reacting to a food over a period of time that reaction would produce physical symptoms and perhaps energy drains. When the energy in the physical body drops, the posture is likely to change reducing support for the spinal column which may result in spinal misalignments. This in turn can cause emotional stress such as irritation, frustration and anger. Very rarely will you find one stress factor present without the other three being apparent in one way or the other. Any or all of those stresses have a significant effect on the neurological system and how it is organised.

For the person with a learning difficulty, the emotional stress release factor will be most valuable.

With almost any form of neurological disturbance comes a form of dysfunction in our ability to process information and thus our learning. Over a period of time we establish beliefs about our ability and often, unfortunately, these are negative beliefs that initiate stress responses, such as fear, anxiety and frustration, all of which get in the way of a clearly organised neurological function.

The technique involves holding neurovascular points or Bennett reflex points* on the forehead. The process is an immensely valuable one for reducing stress yet it one which is so simple that it is often ignored because of that simplicity.

Have the person sit or lie comfortably, preferably with the eyes closed to remove visual distractions and to make it easier for the person to relax.

Now, place the pads of your fingers over what are called the frontal eminences, i.e. the bumps or the most prominent part of the forehead located between the eyebrows and hairline, usually directly in line with the pupils.

To ensure you have the right position put both hands on the forehead with the fingers meeting at the midline above

*In 1930, Dr Bennett, a chiropractor, discovered there were locations on the head which, if held, seemed to influence blood supply to certain organs. In the 1960s Dr George Goodheart, the father of Applied Kinesiology, found he could strengthen a weak muscle by stimulating the appropriate Bennett reflex points. The weak muscles indicate the blood supply of the body is out of balance, with excessive amounts being drawn from other areas to go to areas involved in the fight or flight responses. Holding the Bennett reflex points restored the blood flow to normal and was indicated by a strong locked muscle (P. Dennison, *Switching On*).

the nose. Lay the hands across the forehead with the little fingers on eyebrows (see illustration).

Both middle fingers should just touch in the centre. Use a very light pressure. Hold these points for anything from 30 seconds to as long as 10 minutes to relax the person. Holding these points increases the blood circulation in the forebrain which results in a relaxation response.

This technique can be used as a non-specific technique simply to bring about a relaxed state. However, it may be used much more specifically than if the subject has had a particular group of experiences which have been unpleasant and have caused a degree of emotional stress.

Technique

The Swimmer (Pectoralis Major Clavicular) is the most valuable indicator muscle as it is associated with the stomach meridian which, in turn, is associated with our emotions.

Test the Swimmer for a switched on muscle response and have the person think about the particular instance that causes him stress (reading aloud, anger with parents, peers, etc.) and retest the muscle. On retesting, you will find that the muscle has now switched off.

Hold the points while the person visualises the stress-inducing situation. At times the capillary pulse will be felt on these points. If the situation was a very stressful one, the pulse will beat more heavily and at times even out of synchronicity. Hold the points for 30 seconds to 10 minutes, have the person think of the stressful situation again, and then retest. In most instances the muscle will test switched on. (See John Thie, *Touch for Health* for further information.)

Taking Emotional Stress Release one step further

In many cases, emotional stress factors are very severe and deeply entrenched.

The Swimmer
(Pectoralis Major Clavicular)

Have the person sit down in a comfortable position, and muscle test the Swimmer in the clear. Then retest the Swimmer while the person thinks about the situation that caused the emotional stress. This will switch off the muscle.

Lightly touch the stress release points. We now incorporate the emotional stress release techniques as already outlined with some creative visualisation using the person's imagination to replay the emotionally disturbing scene from the past.

Before starting the actual return to that situation in the imagination, have the person take several deep breaths and as he lets it out, feel the tension leaving his body with each breath.

Have him aware of his body sitting in the chair, what position he is in and if there is any pain or discomfort.

Have him focus on any outside noises he can hear, perhaps the noise of the traffic, perhaps the noise of people in the distance, children in a nearby schoolyard, perhaps the buzzing of an aeroplane overhead or some birds or the wind in the trees outside.

Have him take another deep breath and become aware of any smell in the room.

Have him move his feet and press his toes against the floor.

The purpose of all of these preliminary exercises is to anchor the person in his physical body and to stimulate all his senses.

Ask him to close his eyes and while you place your hands on the frontal eminences ask him to imagine that there is a large television or movie screen and on that screen is the situation that caused the stress. It may have been his standing in front of a classroom of people and having to read. It may have been presenting material that he was aware was not going to be up to standard. It may have been having to write something in front of somebody else and being fearful of making a mistake or being scolded for work that was not up to standard.

Have him observe that whole process in fine detail, having a look at the environment or the room that he was in, the clothes he was wearing, the people who were around as he becomes aware of the feelings that were going on inside at that time and what he might have been saying to them in his mind.

This will allow the person to experience the emotions of the time.

Having had him see those things on the screen and experience the emotional stress, ask him to replay the same scene on the screen, but this time replay with himself in a positive role, so that he sees himself performing confidently, calmly, without stress. He should experience the joy of success and feel what it is like to do something well, to feel confident in his ability.

Let him see himself completing the task and perhaps being congratulated for the standard he has achieved. Then have him imagine that he can stand up and perform that task calmly, with confidence and achieve the best that he is capable of achieving.

Having done that, have him turn the television screen off and reflect on how good it felt to be successful. Now have him focus on the noises outside, the birds, the plane, the people, the children in the playground, have him take in a deep breath and smell the odour in the room. Have him push his feet and toes against the floor and take another couple of large deep breaths and, as he breathes out, allow any residue tension that may have remained to leave his body. Have him feel his body against the chair, have him notice whether the pain that was in his body is still present or if it has passed because of the relaxation that has taken place.

Having done all those things, tell him that, when he is ready, he may slowly open his eyes. Once they are open, have him recall the unpleasant circumstance and retest the muscle response. The muscle response should be switched on.

A few things to remember when performing Emotional Stress Release or using guided imagery

The environment must be quiet, clear and uninterrupted. There should be no possibility of anyone coming into the room. You could ensure this by placing a sign on the door, 'Not to be Disturbed'. Before starting and on completion, it is necessary to anchor the person in his physical body by having him be aware of sounds, his body, noises, smells.

The most important thing is to ensure that you always return the subject to the present and anchor him in his physical body.

Do not interpret anything that has taken place. Just accept whatever comes into the picture or whatever occurs.

The person guiding the visualisation should always use a calm, evenly-modulated voice. The volume should be relatively low but the voice should be clear. A pause of three to five seconds after stating an important point is often appropriate. For example, when you say something to the effect of 'See yourself in the situation up on the screen', pause and allow the person not only to see it but to become involved in the experience.

This can be a very valuable technique because the fears and concerns of past experiences are often the most prominent thought in a learner's mind when he endeavours to do something such as reading, writing or spelling. If the concentration of his focus is on the fear or concern, there is little chance that he will process the information or perform the task as well as if those emotional factors are absent.

Emotional stress release points may be used by students at the beginning of the day prior to school, before spelling tests, before examinations, before having to prepare important assignments, or before homework.

Everyone can benefit from Emotional Stress Release as there are many instances in life where stress occurs. Man has an inbuilt fight or flight mechanism left over from stone age man's need to survive a hostile environment. Modern urban man constantly stresses his system in traffic in racing the clock or dealing with crowds. The fight or flight response is activated (i.e. our blood pressure, heart rate and breathing increases) yet is rarely carried through. Herbert Benson, in *The Relaxation Response*, believes that the constant activating of the fight or flight response without release leads to hypertension with its possible resultant heart attacks and/or strokes and, although the body has a relaxation technique for handling this, the constant stresses in modern life necessitate a stress release method which man can use consciously. He emphasises that this release should include a quiet environment, a repeated word, a passive attitude, and a comfortable position.

Grief is a very common area of stress, as is low self esteem or feelings of inadequacy. Each of these may be assisted by this stress release method.

Emotional Stress Release is an effective technique to use on yourself; you do not need to have someone else present.

In fact, you can create a rather calming, soothing effect and initiate a great degree of relaxation, by holding those points yourself.

Case Study

Jane is a very bright young girl in senior high school years. She is coping with the school work extremely well with very high grades in most subjects. But her handwriting is not nearly up to the standard of any of her other work.

Jane tested positively on virtually all of the tests without indicating any stress factors or any switching off. When asked to write, significant changes occurred. She showed signs of stress, her posture distorted, her hand became very tight when she held the pen and her handwriting was poor.

All the tests were redone, but this time with her holding a pen. She now switched off during the testing procedures, i.e. when testing her 'in the clear', she had tested switched on in nearly all tests, however putting a pen in her hand and retesting her, she switched off in almost all circumstances. Further questioning revealed that earlier in her schooling she had started to write with her left hand and had been forced to change to her right hand while at the same time going from script writing to writing in modified cursive.

This obviously had been a very stressful time for Jane and from then on she had associated the holding of a pen with a very stressful situation. Therefore, any time she held a pen in her hand, she had the same stressed response.

We used the Emotional Stress Release (see chapter Emotional Stress Release). Jane takes herself back in her imagination to the time when she changed hands and when she changed the style of writing. She became quite stressed even thinking about it and on muscle testing she switched off.

The emotional stress release points were held for approximately two minutes. Jane then thought back to the start of that situation and replanned in a positive context so that she could see herself changing hands, writing and changing styles of writing without being stressed. Now, when she thought about the changing over process, she tested switched on.

Jane then repeated the appropriate testing procedures, this time with the pen in her hand. She now tested switched on to each of the exercises.

The next step was to have her do some Horizontal Eights. Her writing then showed a marked improvement.

In a situation such as this, where the stress occurred such a long time ago and was very deeply entrenched, it may be necessary to repeat the process a number of times before the person switches on all the time when holding a pen.

Two other things worthy of mention in Jane's case are these: in writing an essay she had some difficulty putting words on paper. She could plan the essay very clearly in her head but when it came to writing it down, she could not express herself as clearly as she had when verbalising. This again was an indication of the fact that the pen caused a switching off effect to occur.

The second thing was that on testing Jane when spelling orally, she had a very high skill level and was able to spell almost any word without difficulty or hesitation. Conversely, when asked to spell words by writing them, she experienced great difficulty. There were a number of times when she inaccurately spelt words that she had previously spelt quite easily. This again indicated that the pen in her hand caused a switching off effect.

Jane would be a perfect example of a case where Laterality Repatterning, with her holding a pen in her hand, would be appropriate.

The Power of Words

The power of words is probably one of the most underestimated factors in human performance. Certainly the effect of words on the physical body and on the nervous system is generally underestimated.

So that you can experience first-hand the effect of words, we have listed below some words and some alternative words for you to test out.

Testing words

Take a strong indicator muscle, perhaps the Flyer, and test it in the clear, then have the person speak a sentence with the word 'can't' in it (e.g. 'I can't spell' or 'I can't read') and then retest. You will find that the word 'can't' will trigger a switching off effect.

Now, have the person restate the same sentence but substitute the word 'can' or 'will' for 'can't' and retest. This time the effect will be one of switching on.

We have listed below a number of words that we believe can have an adverse effect not only on a person's ability to learn but, more specifically, on his self esteem and on the level of stress he experiences.

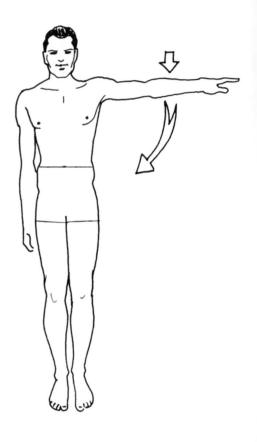

Flyer movement

Words

can't — can	always — most of the time
try — will do	but — and
must — will, choose to	have to — choose to
should — will, won't	cope — manage
never — rarely	right — appropriate
strong — switched on	wrong — inappropriate
weak — switched off	resist — hold

Substitute the negativity of 'don't' with a positive instruction (e.g. 'hold the cup' rather than 'don't drop the cup').

Go through these two columns of words and test some of them. If a word can stop messages passing to and from the brain simply by using that word, imagine what happens if it occurs on a regular basis throughout the day.

Your language is vital in a muscle test — so avoid words that may indicate struggle and failure. The request 'try to hold your muscle/arm' will suggest and also give permission to fail. It will automatically weaken the response. It is better to leave out 'try to' and say only 'hold your arm'.

The importance of choosing appropriate words is discussed in greater detail later in the chapters on self esteem and stress.

The Power of Words

1. Complete this sentence
I must ....
Rewrite it
I choose to ....

2. Complete this sentence
I must ....
Rewrite it
I choose to ....

3. Complete this sentence
I can't ....
Rewrite it
I won't ....

4. Complete this sentence
I can't ....
Rewrite it
I won't ....

5. Complete this sentence
I don't know how to ....
Rewrite it
I want to know how ....

6. Complete this sentence
I shouldn't ....
Rewrite it
I will/I won't ....

7. Complete this sentence
I try to ....
Rewrite it
I will/I won't ....

Important: Read each sentence aloud.

Note — the difference in how you feel when you rewrite each sentence. *Complete these sentences.*

The thing I've realised from writing and rewriting these statements is ....
....

The action I am going to take as a result of realising this is ....
....

This exercise is a valuable one and can be repeated on a regular basis for stimulating a more positive attitude and also for making clear new goals.

Environmental Factors

It is well recognised that the environment affects the neurological system and hence the learning process. For example, the colour of a room may influence behaviour. Pink is now used regularly on the interior of maximum security or high security prisons, because prison authorities say that pink has a soothing effect on the nervous system and hence a soothing effect on behaviour.

Test the individual for his response to a colour by establishing a switched on indicator muscle. Have him look at the colour and retest the muscle. If the colour has an adverse affect, the muscle will test switched off.

Noise is another element that affects us. Its pitch, volume and beat all influence behaviour. The varied impacts of rock-music as opposed to a lullaby are obvious.*

Rock music with its dum-dum-da beat can switch down a person dramatically, as can the loudness of noise or music. Conversely, baroque music can have a calming effect on the nervous system and aid learning.** Because our studies involve a great deal of left brain activity the music keeps our right brain comfortable so we are not overaware of our surroundings and of noises, which make us restless or start daydreaming. Always muscle test the music first and keep it soft enough to be audible but not so loud that it imposes upon our work.

Television's two dimensional screen, flickering light, and silent whine can have a strongly adverse affect on the individual. It also churns out radiation from the back of the set. If you find that watching TV upsets your system sit in the Cook's Technique position.

Synthetics may switch a person off. Place synthetic material (such as plastic) on a person's head then test. Test also with wool, cotton, silk or other natural fibres.

Muscle testing will reveal the effects of all these environmental factors. Test for a strong indicator muscle then subject the person to the environmental factor. For in-

---

*Accelerated Learning see Australian Society of Suggestive-Accelerated Learning and Teaching (SALT) c/- Prof. Gassner-Roberts at Adelaide University.
**For a full discussion of the effects of music, see Ostrander & Schroeder, *Superlearning*.

stance, have him look at different coloured walls, have him work under incandescent light, then natural light, and retest under flourescent light.

The muscle test will give an indication of how that particular environmental factor affects the functioning of the nervous system in that particular individual.

Spelling

English, because of its borrowings from so many languages, is probably one of the most difficult languages to spell. The same sound may be spelt in a number of ways (e.g. sway, weigh, fey, lei) or words spelt similarly are pronounced differently (e.g. cough, tough, bough, though).

We have found visual recall to be an excellent method of learning to spell, not only for those with learning difficulties, but for all people.

Visual recall
Good spellers recall the entire image of the word visually rather than endeavouring to repeat or recall the sound. Poor spellers will benefit from the same technique.

Let us practice visually recalling before we become involved with the strategy of learning to spell. Imagine your front door − look at it. What colour is it? What type of door is it? Does it have some form of locking device or a door knock or bell. Notice how accurately you can visualise the door that you have seen previously. Note that you are not seeing parts of the door − you are seeing it as a total image. You are using the right half of your brain to recall the door − that part of your brain that creates pictures.

To develop the strategy of recalling information in a total picture we are going to visualise images of whole words without breaking them down into their component parts.

A new strategy for better spelling
First obtain 12 sheets of paper or cards approximately 130mm x 210mm (5" x 8") or half a standard A4 size, and on those cards write with a thick felt pen four symbols or shapes (as illustrated).

Do not form words. During the first week or even two weeks of practising the skill, use no more than four letters, numbers, or objects. Write different combinations on each of the 12 cards.
1. Take the card or sheet of paper on which letters are written — turn it away from you so you can't see what is written. Quickly turn the card to face you and immediately turn it away so that you get only a fleeting glimpse of the card.
2. As the card becomes visible to you, blink your eyes as though they are the shutters on the lens of a camera.

3. Put the card out of sight, open your eyes and look up into the *left visual field* to the wall or ceiling. After you have done this several times you will see an image of the word that has just been flashed in front of you. Spell out only those letters that you can see in your imagination.

Eyes looking up into the left visual field

Note: Do not look back to the flashcard to see whether you are correct or not. If we remove the stress involved in getting it right or wrong, we will increase the likelihood of you activating the right half of your brain so that you are able to visualise more effectively.

Repeat this exercise several times with a different card each time.

Ensure that when the card becomes visible you close the shutter of your camera (your eyes) straight away. This does a number of things:

1. It reduces the amount of time you see the card to such an extent that all you are able to do is take a flash image of the whole card.
2. It prevents your eye scanning the line from left to right or from right to left to assess each individual letter. You do not activate the auditory part of your brain which would cause you to subvocalise each letter.

Looking up to the left visual field activates the right

brain — that part that takes in the whole picture and not just the component parts. (Left-handers or people with transposed hemispheres may recall more effectively by looking up to the right visual field.)

Vital point

What we are endeavouring to do here is not to have you spelling accurately straight away, but to teach you the strategy of visually recalling information so that you verbalise only that which you can visualise, not that which you remember.

The next step

The next step is to increase the complexity of the objects.

This exercise needs to be done in pairs. Instead of drawing a number or letter on the card, draw a house with some smoke coming out of the chimney, or draw a tree with a bird in it or draw a square divided into boxes with one of the boxes coloured in.

Now repeat the process outlined above. But this time have your partner hold up the card. Upon identification of the four objects or symbols, have your partner ask questions such as: What can you tell me about the house? how many windows does it have? does it have a chimney? if it has a chimney, is the fire burning or not? if there are puffs of smoke, how many puffs of smoke? if there is a box divided into squares, how many squares are shaded and how many squares are clear? if it is the tree, what can you tell me about the tree?

You will then realise how accurately you can recall fine detail that you were not conscious of when the card was flashed. The technique also develops confidence in recalling information. It is important that the identification of detail is not introduced too early, not until the second or third week of practice of the strategy.

In week three or four, the number of letters could be slowly increased, depending on the person's progress and accuracy. Even at this stage do not indicate whether the person has been accurate in his recall. (See Figure 20 for examples of more detailed flash cards.)

At about week five or six, when the person is becoming proficient and confident, you could start acknowledging and advising the person when he gets the word right. But, instead of saying right or wrong (particularly for people with significant or severe spelling difficulties), give a mark for each attempt — if somebody scores four letters out of five letters, it is 80 per cent accurate. If the person scores three out of five letters, it would be 60 per cent correct. You are focusing on what is correct rather than on what is wrong.

The important thing is the development of the strategy. Once the strategy is learned, the image recalled will be the image that has been seen and, as long as the image is correct, then the spelling of the word will also be correct.

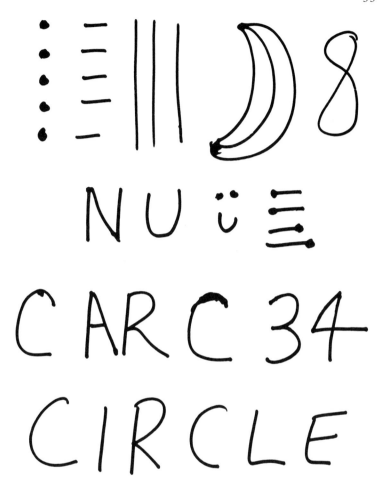

Detailed flash cards

Measuring success

Another method of tes ing accuracy and reaffirming the learner's improvement and ability to recall, is to flash the card and have the person recall the entire image then ask the person to tell you what the third symbol was or perhaps the last or the second last symbol. His success in doing this will reinforce his confidence.

At about week six or seven, it would be appropriate to start introducing words with which the person is familiar. Hold up the word, ask the person to visually recall the word, then to identify the first, third or the fourth letter of the word, or spell the word backwards rather than forwards.

Because spelling is so stressful for many people, it would be useful to use Emotional Stress Release before undertaking these exercises.

It is essential that before words are introduced, the student is accustomed to looking up to the *left visual field* and staying up in the *left visual field*. If, upon flashing the card, the eyes, even for a very short period of time, flash back to the centre or down, then put the card down and flash a new card without having the person recall what he has seen.

This ensures that no subvocalisation is occurring.

Self Esteem

Self esteem, or our self image, plays a significant role in how successful we are. Changing the neurology or changing the mechanism by which we learn is a necessary component in improving learning. But it only handles the mechanics. For true learning to take place and true potential to be achieved, these changes must be accompanied by a positive belief in ourselves.

**Becoming a learner more capable of learning
— becoming a whole person**
The limits we put on our achievements, our abilities, the amount of joy or happiness that we experience, are the primary limits to our success. As we allow our self image to grow, so we allow ourselves to grow.

The self concept or self image is the picture we have of ourselves, of the type of person we are. It is composed of the beliefs and attitudes that have gone before us and is a direct result of everything that has ever happened to us, everything that we have ever said, everything that has ever been said to us.

All of this information is taken into our subconscious mind, a subconscious mind that stores both truth and falsehood, fact and fiction, good and bad, such as all those little things that we say to ourselves every minute of the day — 'Oh, I'm good at that, but I'm not good at this', 'I'm good at mathematics but I'm a terrible speller', or 'I'm not a good public speaker. I'm frightened of crowds' — these contribute to and result from our self image.

All of these things are stored in the subconscious. They are then weighed up and a balance somewhere between the positive and negative ends of the continuum is reached. If we hear from the outside world and also tell ourselves that we are good at mathematics, then we begin to believe it. As a result, stress is reduced and performance improved.

On the other hand, if we constantly hear that we have a problem with mathematics, we soon accept it as the truth, be it accurate or inaccurate, and that becomes the image we have of ourselves. Stress then increases and performance decreases.

Think over your own past and consider what you heard most about yourself. What were the comments of your parents, teachers, friends, or the people around you? Were they mostly positive? Were they constructive? Were they comments that highlighted your strengths? Or were they comments that constantly pointed to problem areas and implied that you were not coping well?

What were the things you were saying to yourself. What were your thoughts? What are the thoughts that go on in your head every day? Imagine that inside of your head is a cassette recorder. What is that cassette recorder playing? Are the cassettes positive or are they negative?

A common saying about computer programming is 'garbage in, garbage out', meaning that if you put garbage into a computer then all that you can get out is garbage. Whereas if you put in accurate data and valuable information, then what you get out of it will be useful and valuable. Our brain is our computer, i.e. what happens to us, what people say to us and what tape recordings we play to ourselves, add up to what we see ourselves to be.

The concepts of improving self esteem and achievement by changing beliefs about ourselves are extensively used in areas of management and of competitive international sport. This is visual image training, i.e. they see the results they want. Motivation and improved belief in oneself invariably results in improvements in one's achievements.

Earlier, in 'The Power of Words', we tested the effects of 'can't' and 'have to', 'should', 'must', 'never' and 'always' and contrasted them with 'can', 'will', 'choose to', 'want to'.

If we hear or use the word 'can't' often enough, soon we believe we are unable to do a task. Yet how many times have we believed, in the past, that we couldn't do something and then found that, after a number of attempts, we have done it?

We must be prepared to make mistakes — and to learn from these mistakes. Only then will we be prepared to take a risk and, by risking, achieve.

Just as we tested in the previous sections of the book the words 'can', 'should' and 'never', you might also test the effects of the words 'right' and 'wrong' and see what happens to your nervous system.

As children one of the first things we learned to do was to walk. When one thinks of the complex combination and co-ordination of switching on and switching off literally hundreds of muscles throughout the body to co-ordinate the action, then learning to walk is an extraordinary accomplishment.

When we first had the innate desire to get up and start moving ourselves about, one of the first things to happen was that we fell down. Had somebody said to us when we fell, 'That's not the way to do it, that's wrong, can't you stand up on your own two feet and move about!' then perhaps the process of walking would have been slowed down. Usually, however, we are strongly encouraged to walk. People say how clever we are. We constantly get up and persist in improving our standing ability and walking. Eventually we learn to walk without thinking about it.

We would like to see this concept applied more frequently to the learning process, i.e. allowing people to make mistakes and drawing from those mistakes the information needed to improve the skill. Each time we walk a little longer we register that as a success and usually people around us tell us we are successful. This continually encourages us to keep going, to stand up again and makes the fall worthwhile. In contrast, in the learning process the mistakes are often emphasised, we are often not applauded for our efforts, nor are we applauded for the risks we take.

The emphasis is on whether what we have done is right or wrong, and not on what we have learned from our attempt.

Positive encouragement is essential for those who have learning difficulties. If, for instance, somebody spells a word and gets five letters right and the sixth letter wrong, then the result is not wrong, it is five out of six. Bring the attention to what has been achieved, rather than what has not been achieved. Constant reaffirming of success increases self image and increases the ability to learn from previous successes and errors.

Whatever the activity, the more often we do it and the more often we focus on the positive aspects of what we have done, the more confident we are going to feel about it and the more likely we are to do it again, improve upon it and learn from our experience.

Self esteem exercises

Exercise 1
The Purpose

The purpose of this exercise is to see the sort of picture we have of ourselves.

Step One
Check the time.

Write down the ten negative words that describe you; words that describe things you are not good at, what you would prefer to see changed, talents or abilities that you lack. Check the time again.

Having completed the list, note the time it has taken you, notice how easy or how difficult it was to come up with words and note what you felt like as you did it.

Step Two
Check the time.

Write down ten positive words about yourself, about talents, skills, qualities you possess. Note the time it takes you to come up with the ten positive words.

Notice how easy or how difficult it was to come up with the ten words and note how you felt. How different was it from writing down the ten negative words.

Remember: There is no right or wrong in this exercise. It merely gives you information about how you see yourself and what you believe yourself to be.

Exercise 2

Step One
Write down five negative statements people have made about you in the past week. They might be things like:

'That's not how to do it, you always do it the wrong way!'
'I don't know why you can't get this right!'
'Don't you understand what I am telling you?'
'You always seem to muck about, don't you?'
'Can't you do better than that?'
'You can't get it right, can you?'

Step Two

The second step is to write down the five pictures those statements brought to mind. Upon completion of that, write down the five feelings that you experienced at that time.

Now repeat the exercise but this time write down five positive comments that you have received in the last week. They might be comments like:

'That's a really good job.'
'I like the way you have done that.'
'That's a great effort, isn't it?'
'That's a big improvement.'
'You really are getting things together, aren't you?'
'That's a very fine effort.'

Having completed that, write down the five pictures that those positive statements produced for you. Then, the five feelings that were associated with those pictures and those words.

Now, having completed both tasks, think back. What was easiest to recall? The positive or the negative words? What did you achieve most of in the last week, positive or negative? What were the pictures that were associated with the words and what were the feelings? What was the end result of the feelings and the pictures, were they positive or negative?

A cautionary note — we are not necessarily saying we can do whatever we want to do today, or even tomorrow for that matter. What we are saying is that our beliefs about our abilities may prevent us from reaching our full potential. It would be untrue to say that tomorrow all of us would be able to speak confidently in front of a large audience; likewise it would be untrue to say that tomorrow each one of us could read 500 words a minute, just as it would be wrong to say that we will all be able to do calculus with great precision. What we are saying is that if we put into the subconscious sufficient information to reinforce the fact that we are capable of more than what we are currently achieving, then we can improve on what we are now achieving.

Each one of us is unique and each of us develops at our own pace. Given the right programming, we will continue to improve and increase the pace at which that improvement takes place by watching and monitoring the words we use on our internal cassette recorder and by being aware of those things which we say to ourselves.

Highlighting the importance of self esteem and particularly the importance of realising we can take control of what goes into our brains is research that has been carried out in an American university, where a group of 100 children were allocated a researcher each. The task of the researcher was to be with the child for the entire day from the time he got up in the morning until he went to bed at night. and to record all the positive and all the negative comments that the child received from the people around him during the day. At the end of the exercise, the 100 researchers added up the totals and drew an average. There were approximately 460 negative comments per day, compared to approximately 75 positive comments per day.*

Bearing in mind the concept 'garbage in/garbage out' and the fact that those children received about six times more negative than positive comments, what is likely to have happened to their self-esteem?

Positive Affirmation

Positive affirmations are positive statements of fact about ourselves. They might be something along the lines of:

* Jack Canfield, 'Loving to Learn and Learning to Love' Seminar, Los Angeles, 1982.

'I am competent and able to learn and work with interest each day'; or

'I am very capable.'

'I'm beginning to recognise the ability and the potential that I have.'

Positive affirmations like these can be developed and used on a regular basis throughout the day to offset the negative programmings that go into the brain's computer.

Remember these important points about positive affirmations.

They need to be: personal

positive

in the present tense

need to have an emotional component

need to be dynamic — they must involve you in doing something

A positive affirmation could be as follows:

'I am improving my reading and writing every day and enjoying it more and more'. When broken down into its component parts, this statement meets the requirements of positive affirmation.

'I'	personal
am improving	present tense, dynamic, active phrase
my reading and writing	personal specific tasks to be accomplished
everyday	reinforces notion of continual improvement
and enjoying it	
more and more	emotional component — reinforces positive nature of the experience

Note that we have not used any words that have negative connotations such as 'no', 'not' or 'but'. Nor have we used any words that make the affirmation conditional upon doing something, such as 'I will improve my writing if I get some assistance'. Words such as 'have to' or 'must' that infer you are being forced into the activity have also been avoided.

Before we construct an affirmation, let us look at some comments, phrases and sentences that spark our enthusiasm and make us feel as if we want to get on and do the job; words, phrases and sentences that make us feel good.

I like the way you did that
That's really great work
You are on target
I didn't think of that, what a good idea
Congratulations
That is very good
Great
I knew you could do it
Go on, keep going, you are on the right track
Oh, good for you
I'm very pleased with what you are doing
That's fantastic
I know you can do it
You are really getting things going now, aren't you?
I think that's the best we have done so far
Things are progressing the way we want them
I like that idea·
I feel really good what's happening with this at present, *how do you feel about it*?
I think that's a big improvement, *what do you think*?
    (by asking, the person is involved in affirming himself and increases his degree of responsibility for his own positive uplift)

Note that in the last two examples we involve the other person. His response will be to affirm the improvement and actively participate in building his own self-esteem. These are the sort of comments that spark people into doing things, take people across their barriers through the risks and fears they have about achieving goals.

A step-by-step procedure to Positive Affirmation

Start by writing the words:

'I am'

and then add two descriptive words, two words that describe you. They need to be positive words:

'I am brave and enthusiastic'

or

'I am sensitive and understanding'

Now add a description of what you are going to do. An example might be:

'I am brave and enthusiastic and working keenly at improving in my work'.

In this example you will notice that all of the requirements of an affirmation are present. It is personal, it is present tense, it is positive, it does have an emotive quality, it is enthusiastic and keen, it is dynamic in its achievement, it has no conditions and it has no negative words or connotations.

Now spend a couple of minutes and read that affirmation aloud to yourself several times and see how it feels. At first it might feel uncomfortable. This discomfort will be an indication that we don't hear positive comments about ourselves as frequently as negative ones and we become comfortable with those things we encounter most often.

Experiment with it and you will find that the more frequently you say it and use it the more comfortable you will feel with it.

Affirmations are a very valuable way of reprogramming our belief in ourselves.

Use the affirmation at times such as walking or travelling when you are not involved in doing specific tasks.

When you feel you are really ready, take the next step towards creating the new image of you — creating the 'true you'. Stand in front of the mirror, look yourself in the eyes and say your affirmation ten times to yourself.

Think of Henry Ford's words: 'Whether you think you can or you can't — you're right'.

The constant use of affirmations will change your thought patterns and will change what you think you can and can't do. If Henry Ford is any guide, positive affirmations will have a very real effect on what you think and, in turn, on what you achieve.

The finishing touch to an affirmation

To give the affirmation meaning and to assist in making it seem more purposeful, write a sentence about the person you want to be. In this sentence include such things as personal qualities or traits, talents, skills, abilities. This is a sentence where you can describe the perfect you.

Over the next month, first thing in the morning, read out aloud the sentence that describes the way you would like to be — the perfect you — and make that your goal. Use the affirmation as the tool for achieving the goal.

The whole exercise will take you no more than a couple of minutes, the results will be worthwhile and will last a lifetime.

Education and EK

Our current educational methods rely upon and reinforce step-by-step, logical, sequential reasoning, that is, activities controlled by the left brain. As doctors, accountants, computer programmers and clerks will testify, our society values such activities and often rewards them handsomely. As artists and writers know, right-brain activities are less valued. Our educational system is not geared to developing creative individuals or Edward de Bono's 'lateral thinkers'. But for students and adults to work at maximum capacity, to achieve satisfaction and fulfilment from their careers, and to develop as fully-rounded, capable individuals, *both* sides of the brain must be utilised.

If schools were to use EK techniques to enhance optimum integrated brain function, students who currently 'hate' school would find many of their problems disappearing. Furthermore, if physical changes were made to the classroom to eliminate factors that inhibit learning (e.g. desks that force students to write to the side; flat desks that force the body to bend over, reducing oxygen flow; fluorescent lighting) then learning would be a more pleasant, less daunting task for many of our children.

We should look again at our grandparents' school methods. Perhaps some of them were not as pointless as we now suppose.

Cross-crawl marching into school (an integrated brain activity), sitting up straight, writing with the face no closer than 12 inches to the table (maintaining oxygen supply and preventing crowding of the stomach and diaphragm), and sitting at a slope desk, all enhance a person's ability to work efficiently. Walking, not riding to school, with a satchell on the back rather than a case in the hand, would positively encourage health, co-ordination, and brain integration.

The old adage 'a healthy mind is a healthy body' is as true today as it was in the past.

Remember: the more you use EK the less you will have to use it.

Reading List

Albrecht, Karl *Brain Power*, Prentice Hall, Englewood Cliffs, New Jersey, 1980.

Barker, Sarah *The Alexander Technique*, Bantam Books, USA, 1981.

Barker, Susan *The Alexander Technique*, Bantam, 1981.

Benson, Herbert *The Relaxation Response*, William Collins & Co., NYC, 1975.

Booth, Dr Audrey *Stressmanship*, Hutchinson, Australia, 1985.

Buzan, Tony *Using Both Sides of Your Brain*, E.P. Dutton, NYC.

Canfield & Wells, 100 Ways to Enhance Self-Esteem in the Classroom.

Dennison, Dr P. *Switching On*, Edu-Kinesthetics, California, 1981.

Diamond, John *Your Body Doesn't Lie*, Harper & Row, NYC, 1979.

Edwards, Betty *Drawing on the Right Side of the Brain*, Fletcher & Sons Ltd, Norwich, B.B., 1979.

Jampolski, G. *Teach Only Love*, Bantam Books, 1983.

Jampolski, Dr J. *Love is Letting Go of Fear*, Bantam Books.

Oich, Roger Von *A Whack on the Back of the Head*, Angus & Robertson.

Paulus, Trina *Hope for the Flowers*, A Newman Book, Paulus Press, N.Y.

Price, Eddie *Is Medicine Really Necessary*, Hale & Iremonger, Sydney, 1985.

Satir, Virginia *Making Contact*, Celestial Arts, California, 1976.

Spugen, S. & Deutsch, G. *Left Brain — Right Brain*, Freeman & Co., SFO, 1981.

Stoner, Fred *The Eclectic Approach to Chiropractic*, F.L.S. Publishing, Las Vegas, Nevada, 1975.

Thie, John *Touch For Health*, Second Back Row Press, 1984, Katoomba.

Tice, Lou *New Age Thinking*, Pacific Institute, Seattle.

Tovey, *Designing with Both Sides of the Brain*, Design Studios, Vol. 5, no.4, October 1984.

Verlee Williams, Linda *Teaching for a Two-Sided Mind — A Guide to Right Brain Education*, Prentice Hall Inc., Englewood Cliffs, New Jersey, 1983.

Ward, A. *Design Cosmologies and Brain Research*, Design Studio, Vol. 5, no.4, October 1984.

Chart Explanation

The purpose of this chart is to allow you, the reader, to have access to a quick and simple way of working with the specific learning disabilities which you want to change.

It will enable you to check which test and exercises you should use when dealing with specific problems.

Because each one of us is uniquely different and will respond differently to different exercises, it is not possible to do one test and say that one particular exercise will make the correction. We may find three people with the same problem, however we may find that each one of them responds to a different exercise.

For that reason we have listed:

1. The 'Signs' of the difficulty.
2. A group of tests by which to check muscle response.
3. A group of exercises which are used for correction. On some occasions it may only take one exercise to make the correction to all of the tests and resolve the problem and on other occasions it may be necessary to do more or all of them.

For that reason it is not appropriate to say for problem number 'one' we use test number 'one' and exercise number 'one'. However what we can say is for problem number 'one' use a particular group of exercises of which some or all will bring about positive change. Details of how to muscle test are on pages 17 to 23.

Signs	Tests	Page	Exercises	Page
Poor Writing (generally)	Have the person write several lines of printing (for reassessing after exercises)	16	Cook's Technique	29
	Have the person write several lines of script or cursive writing (for assessing)	16	Brain Triangle	32
	Muscle Test the 2 parallel lines	27	Zipper	29
	Muscle Test the 'X'	27	Laterality Repatterning	63
	Muscle Test Visual Perception	41	Horizontal Eights	50
			a) with hand; b) with pen	
	Muscle Test Auditory Perception	59		
	Muscle Test Different Posture Positions	35		
	Muscle Test Dominant Eye	45		
	Muscle Test Figure of Eight with both pen and hand	50		
	Muscle Test Cross Pattern Marching	32		
	Muscle Test Homolateral Marching	63		

Signs	Tests	Page	Exercises	Page
Poor Memory and Concentration (generally)	Muscle Test the 2 parallel lines	27	Cook's Technique	29
	Muscle Test the 'X'	27	Brain Triangle	32
	Test Comprehension a) written; b) oral	16	Zipper	29
	Muscle Test Cross Pattern Marching	32	Ear Rolling	60
	Muscle Test Homolateral Marching	63	Cross Pattern Marching	32
	Muscle Test Reading Forwards	24	Laterality Repatterning	63
	Muscle Test Reading Backwards	24	Horizontal Eights a) with pen; b) with paper	50
	Muscle Test Visual Perception	41	Body Eights (Jolly Jumbo)	57
	Muscle Test Auditory Perception	59	Back Tracking	46
	Muscle Test Need for Water	23	Thymus Tapping	40
	Muscle Test Zipper (running up)	29	Emotional Stress Release	78
	Muscle Test Back Tracking	46		

Signs	Tests	Page	Exercises	Page
Hyperactive/Disruptive Behaviour	Muscle Test Zipper	29	Cook's Technique	29
	Muscle Test the 2 parallel lines	27	Laterality Repatterning	63
	Muscle Test the 'X'	27	Horizontal Eights a) with pen; b) with hand	50
	Muscle Test Horizontal Eights (pen and hand)	50	Ear Rolling	
	Muscle Test Auditory Perception	59	Emotional Stress Release	78
	Muscle Test Suspected Food or Chemical Sensitivities	73		
Suspected Food or Chemical Sensitivities	Muscle Test the 2 parallel lines	27	Cook's Technique	29
	Muscle Test the 'X'	27	Laterality Repatterning	63
	Muscle Test Suspected Food and Chemical Substances	73	Abstain from Reactive Foods	73

Signs	Tests	Page	Exercises	Page
Letter Reversal (Classic Dyslexia) — Written — Spoken — Visual, e.g. 'b' as 'd' and 'd' as 'b'	Muscle Test the 2 parallel lines Muscle Test the 'X' Muscle Test Horizontal Eights Muscle Test Reading Forwards Muscle Test Reading Backwards Muscle Test Visual Perception Muscle Test Auditory Perception Muscle Test Cross Pattern Marching Muscle Test Back Tracking Muscle Test Zipper	27 27 50 15 15 41 59 32 46 29	Cook's Technique Zipper Brain Triangle Ear Rolling Horizontal Eights a) with pen; b) with hand Back Tracking Laterality Repatterning Cross Pattern Marching Body Eights Emotional Stress Release Drink Water	29 29 32 59 50 46 63 32 57 78 23

Reading over Punctuation	Muscle Test the 2 parallel lines
	Muscle Test the 'X'
	Muscle Test Cross Pattern Marching
	Muscle Test Homolateral Marching
	Muscle Test Visual Perception
	
	Muscle Test Reading Forwards
	Muscle Test Reading Backwards
	Muscle Test Horizontal Eights
	  a) with hand
		27
		27
		32
		63
		41
		
		15
		15
		50
			Cook's Technique
			Brain Triangle
			Laterality Repatterning
			Emotional Stress Release
			Horizontal Eights
			  a) with hand;
				29
				32
				63
				78
				50

Signs	Tests	Page	Exercises	Page
Arms Slowing Down or Diminishing Range of Movement during Cross Pattern Marching	Muscle Test the 2 parallel lines	27	Cook's Technique	29
	Muscle Test the 'X'	27	Laterality Repatterning	63
	Muscle Test Reading Forwards	15	Horizontal Eights	50
			a) with hand; b) with arm	
	Muscle Test Reading Backwards	15	Cross Pattern Marching	32
	Horizontal Eights	50	Body Eights	57
	a) with hand; b) with arm			
	Muscle Test Cross Pattern Marching	32		
	Muscle Test Homolateral Marching	63		
Reading Deteriorates the Further you Read	Muscle Test the 2 parallel lines	27	Cook's Technique	29
	Muscle Test the 'X'	27	Brain Triangle	32
	Muscle Test Back Tracking	46	Zipper	29
	Muscle Test Visual Perception	41	Laterality Repatterning	63
	Muscle Test Emotional Stress Release	78	Back Tracking	46
	Muscle Test Reading Forwards	15	Emotional Stress Release	78
	Muscle Test Reading Backwards	15	Horizontal Eights	50
			a) with hand; b) with arm	
	Muscle Test Cross Pattern Marching	32		
	Muscle Test Homolateral Marching	63		

Signs	Tests	Page	Exercises	Page
Reading with the Head Moving Back and Forth, Eyes Remaining Still	Muscle Test the 'X' Muscle Test the 2 parallel lines Muscle Test Visual Perception	27 27 41	Cook's Technique Brain Triangle Horizontal Eights a) with pen; b) with hand c) with arm	29 32 50
(Should this not respond to prescribed exercises Chiropractic treatment may be indicated)	Neck Posture Test (e.g. with head down)	35	Body Eights (Jolly Jumbo) Back Tracking once all other corrections are made	57 46
Tracking with Finger when Reading (e.g. Word by Word)	Muscle Test the 2 parallel lines Muscle Test the 'X' Muscle Test Cross Pattern Marching Muscle Test Homolateral Marching Muscle Test Horizontal Eights (pen and hand) Muscle Test Reading Forwards Muscle Test Reading Backwards	27 27 32 63 50 15 15	Cook's Technique Brain Triangle Laterality Repatterning Emotional Stress Release	29 32 63 78

Signs	Tests	Page	Exercises	Page
Head Still with Eyes Jumping and Twitching (If prolonged, may indicate the need for Chiropractic treatment)	Muscle Test the 2 parallel lines	27	Cook's Technique	29
	Muscle Test the 'X'	27	Brain Triangle	32
	Muscle Test Horizontal Eights a) with pen; b) with hand	50	Laterality Repatterning	63
	Muscle Test Reading Forwards	15	Horizontal Eights a) with pen; b) with hand	50
	Muscle Test Reading Backwards	15	Body Eights (Jolly Jumbo)	57
	Muscle Test Neck Posture	37	Back Tracking	46
	Muscle Test Back Tracking	46	Emotional Stress Release	78
Variations in Slope of Writing (Also see Gripping Pen too Tightly)	Muscle Test Visual Perception	41	Move Writing into the Dominant Visual Field	45
	Muscle Test Different Positions in the Visual Field	41		
Variation of Writing (i.e. quality, slope, size and speed) at Different Parts of the Visual Field	See Awkward Posture when Writing		See Awkward Posture when Writing	

Signs	Tests	Page	Exercises	Page
Difficulty Copying from Board	Muscle Test Visual Perception	41	Cook's Technique	29
	Muscle Test the 2 parallel lines	27	Brain Triangle	32
	Muscle Test the 'X'	27	Horizontal Eights a) with pen; b) with hand	50
	Muscle Test Horizontal Eights a) with pen; b) with hand	50	Emotional Stress Release	78
Difficulty taking Dictation	Muscle Test Auditory Perception	59	Ear Rolling	59
	Muscle Test Visual Perception	41	Brain Triangle	32
	Muscle Test Horizontal Eights a) with pen;	50	Cook's Technique	29
	Muscle Test the 2 parallel lines	27	Horizontal Eights a) with pen	50
	Muscle Test the 'X'	27	Emotional Stress Release	78
Good Oral Spelling, Poor Written Spelling	Muscle Test the 2 parallel lines	27	Cook's Technique	29
	Muscle Test the 'X'	27	Brain Triangle	32
	Muscle Test Horizontal Eights a) with pen; b) with hand	50	Alter Posture and Position	
	Muscle Test Writing	46	Horizontal Eights a) with hand; b) with pen	50
	Position and Posture	35		
	Muscle Test Visual Perception	41		

Signs	Tests	Page	Exercises	Page
Good Written Spelling, Poor Oral Spelling (This may indicate a temporomandibular problem if persistant, which would require Chiropractic treatment)	Muscle Test the 2 parallel lines Muscle Test the 'X' Muscle Test Auditory Perception Muscle Test Visual Perception Emotional Stress Response	27 27 59 41 78	Cook's Technique Brain Triangle Ear Rolling Emotional Stress Release	29 32 59 78

Poor Sequencing
  – Counting
  + Putting things in order
  + Phone Numbers
  + Getting the letters
    of words out of order
	See Letter Reversal (Classic Dyslexia)	50	See Letter Reversal (Classic Dyslexia)	50

Poor Spacial Perception
  – Running words together when reading and writing
  – Not starting near the margin
  – Not starting each line under the one above
  – Inability to identify direction
	See Letter Reversal (Classic Dyslexia)	50	See Letter Reversal (Classic Dyslexia)	50

Signs	Tests	Page	Exercises	Page
Good Printing/Poor Script Writing	Muscle Test the 2 parallel lines	27	Cook's Technique	29
	Muscle Test the 'X'	27	Laterality Repatterning	63
	Muscle Test Horizontal Eights a) with pen; b) with hand c) with arm	50	Brain Triangle	32
	Muscle Test Posture	37	Horizontal Eights a) with pen; b) with hand c) with arm	50
	Muscle Test Position of Writing	46	Move Paper	
	Muscle Test Eye Dominance	45	Alter Posture	
			Emotional Stress Release	78
Good Script Writing Poor Printing	As Above		As Above	
Difficulty Expressing Self in Words (orally)	Muscle Test Auditory Perception	59	Ear Rolling	59
	Muscle Test the 2 parallel lines	27	Cook's Technique	29
	Muscle Test the 'X'	27	Laterality Repatterning	63
	Muscle Test Cross Pattern Marching	32	Emotional Stress Release	78
	Muscle Test Homolateral Marching	63		

Signs	Tests	Page	Exercises	Page
Difficulty Expressing Self in Writing (See Game Case Study)	Muscle Test the 2 parallel lines Muscle Test the 'X' Muscle Test Horizontal Eights a) with pen; b) with hand c) with arm Muscle Test Visual Perception	27 27 50 41	Cook's Technique Laterality Repatterning Brain Triangle Horizontal Eights a) with pen; b) with hand c) with arm Emotional Stress Release	29 63 32 50 78
Fidgeting, Foot Tapping or Leg Swinging during Reading, Writing or Listening	Muscle Test Zipper Muscle Test the 2 parallel lines Muscle Test the 'X' Muscle Test for Food Sensitivity Muscle Test Need for Water	29 27 27 73 23	Zipper Laterality Repatterning Food Sensitivity Water	29 63 73 23